T0341933

Listening to Islam

A man in Damascus gave some money to four colleagues – a Persian, an Arab, a Turk and a Greek. The Persian said, 'Let us spend this on *angur*.' 'No,' said the Arab. 'I want to spend all the cash on *inab*.' The Turk made his own demand; 'The money must be spent on *'uzum*.' The Greek shouted above the hubbub, 'We must buy *istafil*.' Now they began to fight each other – because they did not know that each one of them was talking about grapes.

Jalal al-Din Rumi, d. 1273

Listening to Islam

With Thomas Merton, Sayyid Qutb,
Kenneth Cragg and Ziauddin Sardar

Praise, Reason and Reflection

JOHN WATSON

sussex
ACADEMIC
PRESS

BRIGHTON • PORTLAND

Copyright © John Watson, 2005, 2013.

The right of John Watson to be identified as Author of this work has been asserted in accordance with the Copyright, Designs and Patents Act 1988.

2 4 6 8 10 9 7 5 3

First published 2005, reprinted 2013, in Great Britain by
SUSSEX ACADEMIC PRESS
PO Box 139
Eastbourne BN24 9BP

and in the United States of America by
SUSSEX ACADEMIC PRESS
920 NE 58th Ave   Suite 300
Portland, Oregon 97213-3786

All rights reserved. Except for the quotation of short passages for the purposes of criticism and review, no part of this publication may be reproduced, stored in a retrieval system, or transmitted, in any form or by any means, electronic, mechanical, photocopying, recording or otherwise, without the prior permission of the publisher.

British Library Cataloguing in Publication Data
A CIP catalogue record for this book is available from the British Library.

Library of Congress Cataloging-in-Publication Data
Watson, John H., 1939–
    Listening to Islam : with Thomas Merton, Sayyid Qutb,
    Kenneth Cragg, and Ziauddin Sardar : praise, reason, and
    reflection / John Watson.
        p. cm.
    Includes bibliographical references and index.
    ISBN 978-1-84519-101-6 (pbk. : alk. paper)
    1. Islam—Essence, genius, nature. 2. Sufism. I. Title.
    BP163.W35 2005
    297—dc22
                                                    2005010342

Typeset and designed by Sussex Academic Press, Brighton & Eastbourne.
Printed and bound by CPI Group (UK) Ltd, Croydon, CR0 4YY
This book is printed on acid-free paper.

CONTENTS

PREFACE

The genius of literary scholarship, the untiring search for knowledge, the excessive violence of terrorism, the interpretation of mysticism and spirituality, the beauty of holiness and the religious manipulation of politics: all these are present in each contemporary faith system. The major faiths, Buddhism, Christianity and Islam, with minority religions like Judaism or Parseeism, all embody these extremes. All faith systems have their holy people just as they have their violent extremists. There are saints, prophets, sages, gurus and enlightened ones. There are also those who kill in the name of their faith.

In this modest text we are invited to listen to Islam through the hearts and minds of four noteworthy writers. Two Christians with a genuine love for Islam are presented here, alongside two Muslims. A reader can listen to two radically different Muslim scholars and two equally distinct Christian thinkers. Sayyid Qutb (1906-66) embodies quiet divergent aspects of Islam. He was an intellectual committed to close literary and theological study of the Qur'an, but by contrast engaged in the harsh religious manipulation of Middle Eastern politics. Ziauddin Sardar (b.1951) is devoted to the untiring search for knowledge both within the context of his own Islamic tradition and in the related fields of science and modern technology. Thomas Merton (1915-68) engaged tirelessly in interfaith dialogue, confident in the belief that there are no paths but love, peace and mercy in any authentic faith system. Kenneth Cragg (b. 1913) is a philosopher–theologian with a profound knowledge of the Qur'an. He is an Arabist who has served Christian communities in the Middle East at different times from 1939 until the present.

Islam deserves to be listened to. Muslims in the great Cairene university of Al Azhar or those living in isolation in Western diasporas know that their faith can only survive if Islam, through them, manifests the essential gift of peace – the eternal *Salaam* of their faith. The same is true of Christianity. For only those who reveal their possession, in however small a measure, of the fruits of the Spirit ('love, joy, peace, patience, kindness, goodness, faithfulness, gentleness, self-control', Galatians 5.22) can persuade others that the life of the spirit is worth living.

Some who call themselves 'religious' in any faith system are bound to constantly fight the faith of another; the engagement may be physical, intellectual or stridently theological. The call of this text is simply to *Listen to Islam through Cragg, Merton, Qutb and Sardar.*

ACKNOWLEDGEMENTS

The complete text of this book was written to provide the foundations for the fourth annual Advent lectures, given separately at the Methodist and Anglican churches in Highcliffe and sponsored by the local ecumenical organisation *Churches Together in Highcliffe, Dorset.* Interfaith dialogue has been the basis of most of the lectures. I am grateful to the local clergy who have supported this work, and especially to The Reverend Robert Manning, the Methodist Minister who has been a loyal sponsor of the lectures. I have given a total of thirty-two lectures since 2001; half of them were devoted to Islam and Middle Eastern Christianity. Donations were given to churches in Egypt and to Medical Aid for Palestinians.

I am grateful to Bishop Kenneth Cragg, Dr. Paul M. Pearson, Director of the Thomas Merton Centre in Bellarmine University, Kentucky and Professor Ziauddin Sardar for their support of this project. Dr. Cragg and Dr. Sardar have not read the chapters devoted to them, but their readiness to be represented in the author's vocabulary is appreciated. The Reverend Canon John K. Byrom of Cambridge read the entire text and provided excellent editorial advice. I am indebted to John Allen who continues to look after my computer.

My greatest single debt in the preparation of this book is to the artist Robert F. Parham, a graduate of the College of Art at Canterbury, Kent. He has provided the four illustrations of Cragg, Merton, Sardar and Qutb. Sincere thanks to my editor Anthony Grahame and the staff of Sussex Academic Press for their enthusiastic support of this project, and to my wife Jacquie who has worked on the proofs. As to mistakes, the usual formula applies; that is, that all those which remain, and all the opinions expressed, are my own.

Listening to Islam

With Thomas Merton, Sayyid Qutb, Kenneth Cragg and Ziauddin Sardar

THOMAS MERTON

Biographical Outline

"The hermit remains there to prove, by his lack of practical utility and the apparent sterility of his vocation, that monks themselves ought to have little significance in the world, or indeed none at all. They are dead to the world, they should no longer cut a figure in it. And the world is dead to them."

Thomas Merton, *The Monastic Journey*

THOMAS MERTON WAS BORN
IN THE BEAUTIFUL LITTLE TOWN
OF PRADES

in the shadow of the French Pyrenees on 31 January 1915. His mother died in 1921 and his father in 1931, so at the age of fifteen he was an orphan. He had been educated at Montauban Lycée in France. His secondary education was in English, at Oakham, a well-known public school in Rutland, England. He entered Clare College, Cambridge as an undergraduate in October 1933. After serious personal problems, which included fathering an illegitimate child, and evident academic failure, Thomas Merton moved to the United States on 29 November 1934. He joined Columbia University in New York in the autumn of 1935, receiving the degree of Bachelor of Arts in 1938 and entering the graduate school of English to write a dissertation on William Blake. He was well known as a writer, had a reputation for self-indulgent behaviour, drunk too much, smoked heavily and pursued numerous young women.

Quite suddenly and unexpectedly, Merton was attracted to two major intellectuals of Catholic Europe: the historians and philosophers Etienne Gilson and Jacques Maritain. The experience was to become an intellectual and inner turning point in his life, and on 18 November 1938 he was baptised in *Corpus Christi* Catholic Church on West 121st Street, New York. He was awarded his master's degree at Columbia in February 1939 and in the autumn of 1940 he became a teacher of English Literature at St. Bonaventure's Franciscan College in Olean. He applied to join the Order of Friars Minor but they rejected him.

Thomas Merton entered Gethsemani Abbey in Kentucky on 10 December 1941. A few days later he was interviewed by the Cistercian Abbot, Dom Frederic Dunne, and was accepted as a postulant choir monk. On 21 February 1942 his head was shaved and he became a Trappist novice. He threw himself into the variant rhythms of manual labour and the devotional life in chapel and cell. He became *Frater Maria Ludovicus* – Brother Mary Louis. His classic tale of conversion to Roman Catholicism became the best seller,

The Seven Storey Mountain, though publication was frequently delayed by censors and only finally appeared on 4 October 1948, the feast of St. Francis of Assisi. The final blazing lines of this biographical classic are perhaps amongst the most famous in the last century's literary Christian classics:

> *"I will give you what you desire. I will lead you into solitude . . . Everything that touches you shall burn you, and you will draw your hand away in pain, until you have withdrawn yourself from all things . . . Do not ask when it will be or where it will be or how it will be: On a mountain or in a prison, in a desert or in a concentration camp, or in a hospital or at Gethsemani. It does not matter. So do not ask me, because I am not going to tell you. You will not know until you are in it.*
>
> *"But you shall taste the true solitude of my anguish and my poverty and I shall lead you into the high places of my joy and you shall die in Me and find all things in My Mercy which has created you for this end . . .*
>
> *"That you may become the brother of God and learn to know the Christ of the burnt men."*

On 19 March 1949 Merton was ordained a deacon and on 26 May 1949 as a priest: Father Mary Louis, OCSO (Order of Cistercians of Strict Observance). Two people, both of whom could not die, became one person, reconciling Father Louis the Trappist monk with Thomas Merton the writer. "Writing was the religion that bound Merton over to his God. He would give birth to God in himself by writing about his need for God to be born in him. Merton became a monk by writing about becoming a monk. He allowed the form of his particular monastic vocation to reveal itself to him in sequences of experience paradoxical to his readers but holding for him a dark clarity. He wrote about silence to become silent." The relationship between monk and writer is most clearly expressed by Merton himself on 27 September 1958: "I am not going to write as one driven by compulsions but freely, because I am a writer, because for me to write is to think and to live and also in some degree even to pray."

In 1961 he was given permission to spend time in a hermitage in the monastery's grounds where he attempted, often unsuccessfully, to perfect the delicate balance between contemplative prayer, the monastic community and openness to the world. In 1965 with the blessing of Pope Paul the Sixth Fr. Louis became a hermit. In his 1968 book *Faith and Violence: Christian Teaching and Christian Practice* he very simply describes his new vocation up in the forest cabin:

> *"My own peculiar task in the church and in my world has been that of the solitary explorer . . . who is bound to search the existential depths of truth in its silences . . .*
>
> *"If contemplation is no longer possible, then man's life has lost the spiritual orientation upon which everything else – order, peace, happiness, sanity – must depend. But true contemplation is an austere and exacting vocation. Those who seek it are few, and those who find it fewer still."*

It was in the hermitage that Merton began to take a long, quiet and critical look at the church and the world: "Fortunately, I have the woods", he said. In the late sixties he accepted an invitation to address an international conference of monks and nuns in Asia. From the date of his departure from San Francisco on 15 October 1968 he began to write a series of 'Asian Notes', which finally became *The Asian Journal*, though he would never complete it. The journal ranges from a most traditional Catholic pilgrimage to the tomb of St. Thomas in Madras, through a down-to-earth visit to the bars of Colombo, and finally to one of his greatest moments of disclosure when Merton approached the statutes of the Buddha at Polonnaruwa:

> *"Looking at these figures, I was suddenly, almost forcibly, jerked clean out of the habitual, half-tied vision of things, and an inner clearness, clarity, as if exploding from the rocks themselves, became evident and obvious . . . I don't know when in my life I have ever had such a sense of beauty and spiritual vitality running together in one aesthetic illumination . . . my Asian pilgrimage has come clear and purified itself. I mean, I know and have seen what I was obscurely looking for. I don't know what else remains, but I have now seen and have pierced through the surface and have got beyond the shadow and the disguise. This is Asia in its purity, not covered over with garbage, Asian or European or American, and it is clear, pure, complete. It says everything; it needs nothing. And because it needs nothing it can afford to be silent, unnoticed, undiscovered. It does not need to be discovered. It is we, Asians included, who need to discover it."*

His premature, accidental death, apparently from electrocution, occurred in Bangkok, Thailand on 10 December 1968. He was flown home to the Abbey of Gethsemani in Kentucky on 17 December where he was finally buried. In a homily to Merton's brethren, Dom Flavian Burns was most truthful: "The world knew him from his books: we knew him from his spoken word. Few, if any, knew him in his secret prayer. Still, he had a secret prayer, and this is what gave the inner life to all he said and wrote. His secret was his secret to himself to a great extent, but he was a skilful reader of the secret of the souls that sought his help . . . we respected him as the spiritual father of our souls."

At the height of his powers, Thomas Merton wrote some of the most profoundly moving work on Buddhism and Taoism, but it was long after his death that it became quite clear to his colleagues, friends and readers that this Cistercian priest was deeply devoted to Islam, most especially to Sufism.

LISTENING TO ISLAM

with

Thomas Merton

"For myself, I am more and more convinced that
my job is to clarify something of the tradition
that lives in me, and in which I live: the
tradition of wisdom and spirit that is
found not only in Western
Christendom but in
Orthodoxy, and
also, at least
analogously,
in Asia and in Islam."

Thomas Merton, *Conjectures of a Guilty Bystander*

LISTEN FIRST OF ALL TO THIS SINGLE SENTENCE,
WHICH HAS A PARTICULAR RESONANCE
IN THE FIRST DECADE OF
THE TWENTY-FIRST CENTURY:

"It seems to me that mutual comprehension between Christians and Muslims is something of very vital importance today, and unfortunately it is rare and uncertain, or else subjected to the vagaries of politics."

We should be forgiven for associating these words with 11 September 2001, or the many other violent events which have followed. Certainly, the unreliable utterances of American and British politicians – with some additional verbal religious frills – are well known. But these words came from a Trappist monk, writing to a Pakistani Sufi scholar on St. Stephen's Day (Boxing Day), 26 December 1962. Over forty years ago, Merton must already have been thinking of the failure of Christian Muslim dialogue because of the brutal force employed in Israel Palestine. The violence continues to the present. Yet Thomas Merton remained, until the end of his life, one who was deeply committed to the possibility of 'mutual comprehension', most especially with his Muslim correspondent Abdul Aziz, who had devoted his life to the study of Sufism.

The etymology of the word *Sufi* remains a mystery for some, though the majority of researchers are more confident of its meaning. The word is more than a thousand years old, and some would therefore say that the prophet Muhammad was the first Sufi. Many believe that the word *Sufi* can be traced to the Arabic word *suf*, pronounced *soof*, which literally means 'wool' and refers to the material from which the simple robes of early Christian desert fathers were made, and which became the dress of the greatest early Muslim mystics. When it is said that 'wool is the garb of animals' the suggestion is that Coptic and Muslim mystics are not trying to copy a herd instinct but rather to live with primitive simplicity. For a minority, *Sufi* is linked with the Greek *Sophia,* alluding to the divine wisdom. Many others believe that *Sufi* has no recognisable etymology at all. A small number of Sufi scholars are convinced that the 'sounds' of the letters s~u~f (*saad, waaw and faa'* – the four-teenth, twenty-seventh and twentieth letters of the Arabic Alphabet) are more important than the generally perceived etymology. In more than one way of prayer, sound influences the brain and the spirit. *Sufi* may, therefore, be a word with many layers of meaning, and we may not need to push every mystic into a too easily defined category. There is a great simplicity and a distressing difficulty in all the words of all the faiths.

What is Sufism? The question is of vital importance for readers of Thomas Merton. It is also the title of an important study by Martin Lings, a distinguished scholar who was keeper of Oriental Manuscripts and Printed Books at the British Museum and British Library. Part of the answer from Martin Lings is both useful and moving:

> *"Most Western readers . . . will have heard quite early in life that 'the Kingdom of Heaven is within you'. They will also have heard the words: 'Seek and ye shall find; knock and it shall be opened unto you'. But how many of them have ever received any instruction in the way of seeking or the art of knocking? And even as these last four words were being written down, it came to mind that they are, in this given context, an answer to the very question put by our title."*

We understand that the one who teaches us to search and to enquire is our Sufi master. In *The Essence of Sufism*, John Baldock teaches that the Sufis do not conform to the "normal expectations of who or what a 'holy man' should be." But a Sufi is one who has mastered his or her ego and realised an advanced state of consciousness. Searching and enquiring are far from being an intellectual exercise: Sufism is a practical path of transformation and fulfilment "which enables us to free ourselves from the veils of the ego", to connect the secret and external worlds and "discover the unified self within". *What is Sufism?* It is the merging of the drop of water – the individual self – with the Ocean of Being, from whence we have all come. Death is to attain that same unification, and that is why Thomas Merton and Abdul Aziz together represent a tradition that encourages us to understand that merging, even before death itself: "Die before you die."

John Baldock offers the clearest précis: "Islam is not an historical phenomenon. It is the timeless art of awakening by means of submission." The Arabic word *Islam* means 'submission', or to be more precise 'the surrender of one's whole being', to the Divine Unity, to the Oneness that is God. It is the surrender of the drop as it becomes one with the Ocean.

In *The Wisdom of the Sufis*, Kenneth Cragg reminds us that the Sufis were "acute critics of the institutions of religion." Throughout their wisdom there recurs the theme of the ever present dangers in forms of observance and ritual: 'The mystic', they said, 'looks for the ocean of love and therefore cares little for the rivers and canals of prejudice and strife.'

It is most certainly true that the primary method of Sufi communication is through stories, which are unconventional and unusual but immensely powerful; offering answers to our condition. Through its stories Sufism escapes from the illusory, and by its encounter with the real it achieves that union with the Lord of all worlds. Kenneth Cragg understands that, "The wisdom of the Sufis lies in finding out the loneliness of the egotistical self and attaining the community of the essential self." The Sufi account of that discovery "is not without conflicts of interpretation" and they "must be left to speak for themselves. What matters is the consensus of their wisdom."

Islam and Sufism are one for Muslims like Abdul Aziz. There is no Sufism without Islam. But in turning to Thomas Merton it is important to separate him from any tendency to confuse rather than to compare faiths. Islam is precisely described as 'the timeless art of awakening by means of submission' with Sufism at its heart.

Thomas Merton was *en route* to Asia just a few weeks before his death and spoke to a group of Catholic sisters in Alaska. He did not write the words that follow. They were recorded by the Alaskan nuns and recovered from their tape recorders after his death. His impromptu comments about Sufism will remain fixed in the mind because he explains Islam as a Christian priest sees it:

> "*Sufism looks at man as a heart and a spirit and a secret, and the secret is the deepest part. The secret of man is God's secret; therefore, it is in God. My secret is God's innermost knowledge of me, which He alone possesses. It is God's secret knowledge of myself in Him, which is a beautiful concept.*

The heart is the faculty by which man knows God and there Sufism develops the heart.

This is a very important concept in the contemplative life, both in Sufism and in the Christian tradition: To develop a heart that knows God, not just a heart that loves God, but also a heart that knows God. How does one know God in the heart? By praying in the heart. The Sufis have ways of learning to pray so that you are really praying in the heart, from the heart, not just saying words, not just thinking good thoughts or making intentions or acts of the will, but from the heart."

We need no further disclosure of Merton's sincere love for Sufi Islam than this, but he has many other necessary things to teach us.

Merton's voluminous correspondence has been widely published in the last three decades. Although his letters to Muslims cannot be compared with the many he sent to fellow writers and monastics, the correspondence concerning Islam is an important resource for anyone attempting to find some positive engagement between Christianity and Islam. The brief correspondence with the distinguished Iranian academic Seyyed Hossein Nasr has not been published; though it was Professor Nasr who had planned Merton's early 1969 visit to Iran from Thailand, which should have led the Cistercian monk to a deeper understanding of the many expressions of Sufism in 'Persia'. In *Merton and Sufism: The Untold Story: a Complete Compendium*, Seyyed Hossein Nasr gave an appreciation of Thomas Merton that cannot pass unnoticed:

"Let it be said first of all that Merton's knowledge of Sufism was authentic and genuine and not derived from either sentimental pseudo-Sufi writings nor from dry scholarly analyses of Sufism by a certain class of scholars who are interested in Sufism only if the spirit of Sufism is taken out of it, scholars who are much more at home dissecting cadavers than studying living beings . . .

"What would have happened if Merton had been able to come to Persia and to continue his study of Sufism, only Heaven knows. In any case that was not to be. Perhaps he would have written major works of Sufism in its relation to Christian spirituality. But even what he did write and the thoughts that he did express to friends reveal the inner sympatheia he had towards the Islamic spiritual universe."

Merton's briefest published correspondence concerning Islam was that with Martin Lings, the author of many important texts on Islam and Sufism, who sent a copy of his book *A Moslem Saint of the Twentieth Century (Sheikh Ahmad Al-Alawi, 1961)* to Gethsemani. Ahmad al-'Alawi (1869–1934) was an Algerian Sufi master who founded a *tarîqah*: a branch of the Darqasi–Shîdiliyya Sufi Order. Merton was in contact with members of this congregation. *Tarîqah* is similar to many Western spiritual traditions: it is the journey from outer, formal reality to inner spiritual freedom. Al-Alawi, Lings and Merton were aware of the same spiritual path. Father Louis (T.M.) reviewed the book for the publication *Collectanea Cisterciensia* (No. 27, 1965) which is published in French for the Cistercians. In a letter of 24 April 1965 Merton gave Lings his appreciation: "The book was an inspiration to me and I often think of this great man with veneration. He was so perfectly right in his spirituality. Certainly a great saint and a man full of the Holy Spirit. May God be praised for having given us one such, in a time when we need many saints."

After Merton's death the review copy was found in his personal library in the forest cabin. It was heavily scored throughout. Marginal marks appeared everywhere. Gray Henry, in her appraisal of Merton's private copy, understands the markings as the indicators of his personal response to Islamic mysticism. The first passage marked by Merton comes from an early eighth-century saint, Hasan al-Basri: " 'He that knoweth God loveth Him, and he that knoweth the world abstaineth from it,' and the saying of another early Sufi: 'Intimacy (*uns*) with God is finer and sweeter than longing.'"

The final evocative phrase marked by Merton in the biographical study of Sheikh Ahmad Al-Alawi possibly comes from a *hadith* (a tradition, saying or anecdote of the prophet Muhammad):"The dearest of men unto Me (God) is he who maketh Me dear unto men, and maketh men dear to me." Abdul Aziz and Ahmad Al-Alawi belong with Thomas Merton in Surah *Al-Ma'idah* (The Banquet, or The Table Spread) 5.82–3: "Nearest among them in love to the Believers (Muslims) will you find those who say, 'We are *Nasara* (Christians)': because amongst these are men devoted to learning (priests) and men who have renounced the world (monks), and they are not arrogant. And when they listen to the revelation received by the Messenger (Muhammad), you will see their eyes overflowing with tears, for they recognise the truth." (Abdullah Yusuf Ali). It can be no surprise that Merton's review of the book contains the words, "This grand Sheikh had even a certain Universalist and ecumenical spirit . . . It is thus our part, in the face of Islam, to be ready to understand everything which is authentic in the aspirations of Sufism."

Another of Merton's Muslim correspondents was Dr. Reza Arasteh who related Eastern and Western psychology to the mysticism of the great Muslim mystic Rumi. But the must influential correspondence was that with Abdul Aziz, published in *The Hidden Ground of Love*, whose letters not only sparked Merton's interest in Sufism but from whom Merton learnt most at a personal level. Here is the Trappist addressing the Sufi in November 1960:

> *"As one spiritual man to another (if I may so speak in all humility), I speak to you from my heart of our obligation to study the truth in deep prayer and meditation, and bear witness to the light that comes from the All-Holy God into this world of darkness where he is not known and not remembered. The world we live in has become an awful void, a desecrated sanctuary, reflecting outwardly the emptiness and blindness of the hearts of men who have gone crazy with their love for money and power and with pride in their technology. May your work on the Sufi mystics make His name known and remembered, and open the eyes of men to the light of His truth."*

One year later, Merton had read many more books about Islam, and was especially impressed with Titus Burckhardt – author of fifty books on Sufism and mysticism. Burckhardt and others had 'opened up new horizons for him':

> *"I am tremendously impressed with the solidity and intellectual sureness of Sufism. There is no question but that here is a living and convincing truth, a deep mystical experience of the mystery of God our Creator Who watches over us at every moment with infinite love and mercy. I am stirred to the depths of my heart by the intensity of Muslim piety toward his names, and the reverence with which he is invoked as the 'Compassionate and the Merciful.' May He be praised and adored everywhere forever."*

In this comment, Merton is aware of the central Sufi experience of *dhikr*, which is the recollection, or remembrance of God. God speaks to Muslims in the Qur'an 2:152, 'Remember me and I shall remember you' (Asad). 'So remember me; I will remember you' (Haleem). 'Remember me: I will be mindful of you' (Cragg). 'Then you remember me; I will remember you' (Aziz). The practice of *dhikr* refers to the invocation of one of the Divine Names, and other related formulae. *Dhikr* is not unrelated to the Jesus Prayer, in the *Way of the Pilgrim*, or the use of the rosary, for prayer beads are indeed used in Sufi Islam. Because the names of God form a cornerstone in Islamic spirituality, and provide a central means of worshipping God and invoking his presence, they are repeated in ritual form, out loud or in the mind, with special breathing and physical movement, but it is perhaps the inner sense of remembrance that is central for the Trappist Merton or the Sufi Aziz.

In 2005 it will be noted that the Orthodox Christian composer Sir John Tavener is to hear the first public performance of his new choral work based on the ninety-nine names for God in Islam. The work will be sung in Arabic. In an interview with *BBC Music* magazine in Autumn 2004, the composer said that each divine name is set to an original theme. There is no musical repetition. Tavener is responding spontaneously to the Arabic words, because the ninety-nine names in English lack the timbre enjoyed in the language of the Qur'an: "I mean, when you say the names in English – the Vast, the All-Merciful, the Punisher – they seem ridiculous. In Arabic they have a resonance." The composer is writing what he describes as an Orthodox Christian's affirmation of Islam, rather than 'the terrible negations' that he sees everywhere. Tavener the Greek Orthodox is not unlike Merton the Catholic: 'I do pray within my heart all the time.' One further work by Tavener reflects the composer's urgent sense of inter-faith dialogue and relates firmly to the Merton–Aziz correspondence. These three men – Catholic, Muslim and Orthodox – together recollect the name of God. They speak as one person of Sufi *dhikr*, which is that recollection, remembrance and commemoration of the Divine Name. In both faith systems the name must be taken into the heart. In classical Christian Orthodoxy the Jesus Prayer is simple: "Lord Jesus Christ, Son of God, have mercy on me a sinner." The same tradition would stand here as in Sufi *dhikr*: you must be silent yourself and let the prayer speak. John Tavener has set the Jesus Prayer in four languages: Coptic, English, Greek and Church Slavonic. *The Prayer of the Heart* (The Jesus Prayer) was performed in 2003 by the Icelandic singer Björk and the Brodsky Quartet. The composer describes the performance as savage, untamed, spontaneous and simple, but 'above all filled with a sense of remembrance'. Music has the power to evoke recollection and celebration. Perhaps the silence between the notes has a similar eloquence.

Dhikr as the remembrance of God, with other elements of classical mysticism, is also related to the concept of *fana'* which is the passing away, annihilation or extinction of the self within the love of God. On the Sufi path, the final stage of *fana'* is described as *fana' al- fana'*, perhaps best expressed as *the passing-away-of-passing-away*, when the mystic is no longer even conscious of having attained *fana'*.

Merton understood the Islamic concepts of *dhikr* and *fana'* not only as a scholar and writer but also as one who lives within these models. Most eloquently in *The Hidden Ground of Love*:

> *"My prayer tends very much toward what you call fana'. There is in my heart this great thirst to recognise totally the nothingness of all that is not God. My prayer is then a kind of praise rising up out of the centre of Nothing and Silence. If I am still present "myself" this I recognise as an obstacle about which I can do nothing unless He himself removes the obstacle. If he will he can then make the Nothingness into a total clarity."*

Since 11 September 2001, there has been a limited commitment to interfaith *dhikr*. Only a few Christians and Muslims are aware that both might learn to be present before God, when freed from overbearing intellectual and conceptual control. Merton and Aziz adopted the practice of praying for one another at the dawn of each day. Dawn is one of the daily moments of Muslim *Salat,* in which ritual prayer is offered five times every day. The earliest offering is known as *Salat al-Farj,* to be said when the dawn has broken before the actual sunrise. The Qur'an invites us to establish worship at the two ends of the day, and in the parts of the night close to them:

> *"And be constant in praying at the beginning and the end of the day, as well as during the early watches of the night: for, verily, good deeds drive*

away evil deeds: this is a reminder to all who bear God in mind." (Surah Hud 11.114. Asad)

On any morning, in a city like Cairo – known as the city of a thousand mosques – the *adhan* (the call to prayer) at *Salat al-Farj* is a moment of mystical *glossolalia*, when the city hums and sings with devotion to God. For any Christian visiting the Middle East *Salat al-Farj* can be a moment of disclosure. Thomas Merton referred to the hour of the dawn as the time "when the world is silent and the new light is most pure, symbolising the dawning of divine light in the stillness of our hearts . . . This represents for us the moment of the nearest presence of God in our lives: He is present at all times, but we believe that at this time His mercy and His bounty express themselves most fully towards us." Abdul Aziz also decided to pray for Merton on *Laylat al-Qadr* (the Night of Power), when the Qur'an came down into the mind and upon the lips of Muhammad.

In a passage that retains significance for all who trace the borders of interfaith contacts, Merton wrote to Aziz on 13 May 1961, emphasising their shared priorities:

"He alone is Real, and we have our reality only as a gift from Him at every moment. And at every moment it is our joy to be realised by Him over an abyss of nothingness: but the world has turned to the abyss and away from Him Who Is. That is why we live in dreadful times, and we must be brothers in prayer and worship, no matter what may be the doctrinal differences that separate our minds."

Merton sounds like a prophet and visionary speaking after the invasions of Afghanistan and Iraq. How very different he is from contemporary 'Christian conservatives' of the West. In August 1963 Abdul Aziz wrote with enthusiasm about a statement of Pope Pius XI (1857–1939) – cited in *L'Ultima*: anno. viii, Florence 1954 – where His Holiness is reported to have told Cardinal Facchinetti, the apostolic delegate to Libya: "Do not think you are going among infidels. Muslims attain to salvation. The ways of providence are infinite." When Aziz invited Merton to comment on the words of Pope Pius, the Trappist replied in a remarkably straightforward way: "I have no doubt in my mind whatever that a sincere Muslim will be saved and brought to heaven, even though for some reason he may not subjectively be able to accept all that the Church teaches about Christ."

In common with many Christians who have a particular interest in Islam, Father Louis OCSO of Gethsemani frequently focused upon the three 'Abrahamic faiths', though it seems that he was blissfully unaware of the concept of abrogation employed by some schools of Muslim thought in relation to Judaism and Christianity. In Islamic Theology and Ethics *the concept of abrogation* refers to the notion that the later, institutional Quranic revelations of Medina repeal, annul and abolish the earlier, pacific and ecumenical Meccan revelations, thus undermining many peaceable acknowledgements of Christianity and Judaism given in the earlier ministry of the prophet Muhammad. Mecca was a place of martyrdom, urging and proclamation; Medina a place of politics with the exercise of sovereign power. The religious reality belongs to Mecca, the place of pilgrimage to which every *kiblah* in the world points but there is no guarantee for Medina's politics. Kenneth Cragg, a key Christian scholar of Islam has noted that 'there can be no doubting the priority of the Meccan world'. But it was Fazlur Rahman, a prominent Muslim academic, who marked the distinction between Mecca and Medina by writing of the need to 're-invigorate the elements that are intrinsically Islamic.'

There is no evidence that Merton grasped any of the essential conflicts within Islam, but he was a courageous thinker whose *concept of salvation* sometimes seems like a balancing act: a Catholic monk and a Universalist trembling on the same tight rope. In a letter to Abdul Aziz of 28 June 1964, Merton develops his earlier interpretations:

> "There is and can be no question in my mind that every sincere believer in God, no matter what may be his affiliation, if he lives according to his belief, will receive mercy and, if needed, further enlightenment. How can one be in contact with the great thinkers and men of prayer of the various religions without recognising that these men have known God and have loved Him because they recognise themselves loved by Him? It is true that there are different ways to Him and some are more perfect and more complete than others. It is true that the revelation given to 'the people of the book', Christians, Jews and Muslims is more detailed and more perfect than that given through natural means only to other religions."

The study of Muslim–Christian relations urgently requires examination in both communities: without an interior exchange the dialogue will have no future. Academics who give papers to each other rarely sit together with the sense of being still before God. Liturgical prayer – the *Bismillah* and 'Our Father' – may be said in opposition, but thirty years after the close of the Aziz Merton correspondence a spiritual friendship springs from the pages. Professor Sidney Griffiths is correct and challenging in his commentary on their exchanges: "From the perspective of interreligious dialogue on an experimental basis" this correspondence "is still unique." The challenge lies in Griffiths's last three words – "is still unique". Without dialogue on an experiential basis there will be no real dialogue at all.

Merton was a very private person, especially in personal prayer. Fr. Basil Pennington a fellow-Trappist tells us that "nowhere in the writings he published have we found a really personal expression of his own use of prayer." Merton's autobiography is amongst the finest Christian books of the twentieth century. His journals were tightly edited, but it was in his posthumously published letters that he was revealed as most open, especially with those who shared a deep spiritual bond, most significantly those from other religious traditions. It was in the following letter to Abdul Aziz that Merton gave his fullest, and perhaps only, description of his way of private prayer and meditation:

> "Strictly speaking I have a very simple way of prayer. It is centred entirely on attention to the presence of God and to His will and His love. That is to say that it is centred on faith by which alone we can know the presence of God. One might say that this gives my meditation the character described by the prophet as 'being before God as if you saw Him'. Yet it does not mean imagining anything or conceiving a precise image of God, for to my mind this would be a kind of idolatry. On the contrary, it is a matter of adoring Him as indivisible and infinitely beyond our comprehension, and realising Him as all . . . If I am still present 'myself' this I recognise as an obstacle. If he wills he can then make the Nothingness into a total clarity. If he does not will then the Nothingness actually seems it to be an object and remain an obstacle. Such is my ordinary way of prayer or meditation. It is not 'thinking about' anything but a direct seeking of the Face of the Invisible. Which cannot be found unless we become lost in Him who is Invisible."

Merton the man of prayer is never far from Merton the poet because his poetry so often connects with his prayer. Seven of his poems (*The Collected Poems of Thomas Merton*, 1940–77) are eloquent testimonies of his Christian devotion to Islam and Muslim people. A review of Merton as poet would require much space but it is true that there are lines in all his 'Islamic' poems that echo the prayer life of the monk of Gethsemani, Kentucky. He is perhaps at his most eloquent when he writes as if he were a Sufi:

> *To belong to Allah*
> *Is to see in your own existence*
> *And in all that pertains to it*
> *Something that is neither yours*
> *Nor from yourself,*
> *Something you have on loan:*
> *To see your being in His Being*
> *Your substance in His Substance,*
> *Your strength in his Strength.*

Nearly forty years ago (7 November 1965) Merton wrote to his foremost Muslim correspondent: "We must humble our hearts in silence and poverty of spirit . . . and work that men's hearts may be converted to the ways of love and justice, not of blood, murder, lust and greed. I am afraid that the big powerful countries are a very bad example to the rest of the world in this respect." It is sad that Muslim Christian dialogue today is buried in war. Academic debate, cultural exchange and institutional conversations do happen but they are peripheral to the current problem, and lack numinous depth. Transfiguration comes in the hidden symposium of Dawn where mystic and monk met. In their thirst, assuaged only by the waters of stillness, Trappist Merton and Sufi Aziz recovered Peace. The great Silence at the heart of the religions is an enigma, but it is also known as a Presence: 'It was We who created man, and We know what dark suggestions his soul makes to him: for We are nearer to him than his jugular vein' (Aziz). 'We created man – We know what his soul whispers to him: We are closer to him than his jugular vein' (Haleem). 'We created man: We know the very whisperings within him and We are closer to him than his jugular vein' (Cragg). 'It is We who have created man, and We know what his innermost self whispers within him: for We are closer to him than his neck-vein' (Asad) (Surah 50.16 *Qaf*). Even within the intimacy of this Presence there is between Christian and Muslim a human element. Dialogue must mean inclusion within the life and spirit of another than oneself, and both the Cistercian and the Sufi in our story reach to the Silence of Peace that is within and beyond. This does not happen in institutional religion, but Thomas Merton and Abdul Aziz could have known each other in the words of Jalal al-Din Rumi (d. 1273), who was most certainly an exceptional Sufi source for both of these partners in prayer:

The Man of God is drunk without wine:
The Man of God is full without meat.
The Man of God is rapturous, amazed:
The Man of God has neither food nor sleep.

The Man of God is a king beneath a lowly cloak:
The Man of God is a treasure in a ruin.
The Man of God is not of wind and earth:
The Man of God is not of fire and water.

The Man of God is a sea without a shore:
The Man of God rains pearls without a cloud.
The Man of God has a hundred moons and skies:
The Man of God has a hundred sunshines.

The Man of God is wise through Truth:
The Man of God is not a scholar from a book.
The Man of God is beyond faith and disbelief alike:
For the Man of God what 'sin' or 'merit' is there?

The Man of God rode away from Non-being:
The Man of God has appeared, sublimely riding.

The Man of God Is – Concealed – O Muslim!
Search for, and find – The Man of God.

SOURCES FOR THE STUDY OF THOMAS MERTON

A. J. Arberry *Discourses of Rumi*, S. Weiser, New York, 1972.
Ed. Rob Baker and Gray Henry, *Merton & Sufism. The Untold Story. A Complete Compendium*, Fons Vitae Kentucky, 1999.

John Baldock, *The Essence of Sufism*. Eagle Editions Ltd., London 2004.

Kenneth Cragg, *The Wisdom of the Sufis*, Sheldon Press, London 1976.

Robert Ellsberg, *All Saints. Daily Reflections on Saints, Prophets, and Witnesses For Our Time*, Crossroad Publishing, New York 1999.

Jim Forest, *Living With Wisdom: a life of Thomas Merton*, Orbis Books, New York 1991.

Timothy Freke *Rumi Wisdom*, Godsfield Books, Hampshire 2000.

Martin Lings, *What Is Sufism?* George Allen & Unwin, London 1981.

Thomas Merton, *The Seven Storey Mountain*, Harcourt Brace 1948. Trustees of the Merton Legacy Trust, Kentucky, 1976.

——, *Faith and Violence. Christian Teaching and Christian Practice.* University of Notre Dame Press, Indiana 1968.

——, *Thoughts on the East*, Ed. George Woodcock, Burns and Oates, London 1996.

——, *The Wisdom of the Desert*, Hollis & Carter, London 1961.

——, *The Collected Poems*, New Directions, New York 1977.

Michael Mott, *The Seven Mountains of Thomas Merton*, Houghton Mifflin, Boston, 1984.

R. A. Nicholson, *The Mevlana of Jalal al-Din Rumi*, trans. 'Our Master'. Unwin, London 1950.

M. Basil Pennington, *Thomas Merton. My Brother*, New City Press, New York 1996.

Edward Rice, *The Man in the Sycamore Tree. The Good Times and Hard Life of Thomas Merton*, Doubleday Image Books, New York 1972.

Ed. Oliver Roland, *Kirche im Dialog: Anthologie fur Religion 3,1.* Azur Verlag, Mannheim 2003.

Anne Marie Schimmel, *Rumi's World*, Shambala, Boston 2001.

Ed. Wm. H. Shannon, *The Hidden Ground of Love. The Letters of Thomas Merton on Religious Experience and Social Concerns*, Collins, Flame, London 1990.

——, *Witness to Freedom. The Letters of Thomas Merton in Times of Crisis*, Farrar-Strauss-Giroux, New York, 1994.

Ed. Angus Stuart, *The World in My Bloodstream. Thomas Merton's Universal Embrace*, Conference papers 2002, Three Peaks Press, Wales 2004.

Sayyid Qutb

Biographical Outline

"One individual struggles but achieves no more
than Hell, and another makes every effort to
achieve Paradise. Everyone is carrying his
own burden and climbing his own hills
to arrive finally at the meeting place
appointed by God, where the
wretched shall endure their
worst suffering while the
blessed enjoy their
never-ending
happiness."

Sayyid Qutb, *In the Shade of the Qur'an*

SAYYID QUTB
WAS BORN IN THE VILLAGE
OF MUSHA NEAR ASSYUT
IN UPPER EGYPT

on 9 October 1906. At that time the rural community was a tra-ditional Egyptian mix of Muslims and Copts. Qutb always associated his neighbourhood with rural superstition and primitive customs, but his father was active in the secular national Party (*Hizb al-Watan*) and an enthusiastic subscriber to the party's jour-nal *al-Liwa'* (The Standard). Sayyid Qutb's education began at home, where as a child he memorised the Qur'an. In 1930 he moved to *Dar al'Ulum* (House of Science), a teacher training col-lege in the Egyptian capital, graduating in 1933 at the age of twenty-seven. He continued to study at Cairo University. The Ministry of Education eventually appointed Qutb an inspector of schools. In the 1930s and 1940s he attempted to write a novel *Ashwak* (Thorns). It was a limited success, but he went on to pro-duce some significant and lucrative literary criticism. He became a habitué of the literary café society of the Egyptian capital where he encountered major literary figures like 'Abbas Mahmoud al-'Aqqad (1889–1964) and Taha Hussein (1889–1973). They were important influences on him. It has often been reported that he was, during this same period in Cairo, a friend of the Nobel Prize-winner Naguib Mahfouz (b. 1911), though the association seems unlikely in the light of the Nobel laureate's radical literary output, and in view of the fact that one of Sayyid Qutb's later disciples attempted to kill the great novelist. Tragically, another of Qutb's followers succeeded in assassinating President Anwar Sadat on 6 October 1981. Sayyid Qutb may have damaging associations with insurgency but his literary reputation has survived.

Qutb's earliest association with politically active cells began when he joined popular protests against the British for their abuses of the native population in Palestine and their support of Zionist occupation of that country from 14 May 1948 onward. Immediately before the Egyptian Revolution of 1952 under General Muhammad Naguib, and despite being a government employee, Sayyid Qutb became an agitator against the rule of King Farouk the First, who finally fell from power on 26 July 1952. But earlier – not long after the Second World War and just after the Palestinian débâcle – Qutb was awarded a major government research scholarship to study in the United States. The Ministry of Education hoped that his postgraduate study of Education from 1948 to 1951 in Washington, Colorado and California would widen his horizons and limit his criticisms. It did not. His loathing for American 'infidel' society became even stronger and for the rest of his life he would rewrite the Qur'an and the history of Islam as his own autobiography. Qutb hated Western civilisation and its culture, making it clear that he regarded the American way of life as sinful and degenerate, addicted to sexual promiscuity. He was himself very clearly sexually frustrated and recounted many sexually charged encounters with modern Cairene and American women. Commenting upon the use of church halls in the United States he noted, "The dance is inflamed by the notes of the gramophone, the dance-hall becomes a whirl of heels and thighs; arms enfold; hips, lips and breasts meet, and the air is full of lust."

Sayyid Qutb's commentary may help to explain why his recent adherents in Indonesia regarded the clubs in Bali as legitimate targets (2003). When he commented on modern American music in general, but of Jazz in particular, he described the latter as a "type of music invented by Blacks to please their primitive tendencies." In his time at Colorado State College of Education, where he declined an invitation to obtain further postgraduate qualifications, Sayyid Qutb remained obsessed with sexuality and American society. He had an *occidentalist* view of the West: the standpoint of one who looks through tinted glasses and accepts the narrowest view of the western world. He is not unlike the *orientalist*, who viewed the Middle East and Islam with similarly narrow preconceptions. Qutb never visited Europe.

On his return to Egypt in 1951 Qutb became the most important ideologue of the Muslim Brotherhood (*al-Ikhwan al-Muslimin*). At first he maintained close relations with General Muhammad Naguib, Colonel Gamal 'Abd al-Nasser, Colonel Anwar Sadat and the Free officers who led the coup of July 1952, but Qutb's attacks upon Western values, the democratic system, socialism – and especially upon 'the American way of life' – were so extreme that he was required to resign from the Ministry of Education in 1952. From that moment he devoted his life to the Muslim Brotherhood and he began his sustained attack on the new leaders of the Egyptian National Revolution. Although he criticised the degeneracy of western society, Qutb claimed that the rulers of his homeland, Saudi Arabia and most of the Middle East, were not true Muslims, because they had failed to implement the *Shari'a*, the religious law of Islam. In his view, corrupt westernised rulers, who were in effect pagans, governed the Muslim world. Qutb was certain that Egypt and America were alike because of the disintegration of their material and spiritual lives. Whilst it should always be recalled that this scholar was a skilful, affecting and sometimes subtle thinker it cannot be forgotten that he became the ideological guide for terrorism and the cult of death. He liked to mock every other believer – Christian, Jewish or Muslim – for their 'passion to be alive'. Muslims and many others see him as one of the 'fathers of suicide bombing'.

Jihad has a range of meaning in Islam. It can be a personal religious struggle, against greed, self-regard and voracious physical needs. *Jihad* might mean the need for communal effort and growth. *Jihad* could also be a personal or collective intellectual struggle. But *Jihad* can also most definitely be a 'holy war' – a defensive strategy to preserve Islam. For Qutb it was above all a war against infidels everywhere – the West most certainly, Jews in particular, but the spiritually ignorant in Egypt and the Middle East above all. In this context it is not surprising that the Muslim Brotherhood made an attempt on Nasser's life on 26 October 1954. Qutb was sentenced to twenty-five years hard labour, and was imprisoned at the Tora prison, operated by State Security Intelligence services and lying to the south of Cairo between Maadi and Helwan. The prison is located in a marble quarry. The name of the prison came from the *Keter Torah*, a centre of Judaic scholarship and rabbinical training. Some Coptic Orthodox Christians have been incarcerated at the Tora and torture was common there.

Qutb served a ten-year prison term. Employing all his exceptional literary and intellectual skills, he devoted a decade of detention into writing himself into the Qur'an, moving through aesthetics, with his great passion for the Arabic language, into the world of political action and violence. The psychology of the writer should not be defined solely in political terms for it is clear from much of his later work that Qutb suffered from deep sexual anxiety, even though his politics and his personal brand of literary funda-mentalism have been allowed to dominate his biography. On 30 August 1965 the Egyptian Government exposed a new plot against President Gamal 'Abd el-Nasser. Sayyid Qutb had been released from prison just a few months earlier but he was amongst those found guilty of treason. He was imprisoned with his younger brother Muhammad Qutb who had also joined the Muslim Brotherhood.

Jahiliyya is a classical Islamic term for the period of paganism in Arabia before the coming of the prophet of Islam with his message. When we turn and 'listen to Islam' through Sayyid Qutb we shall need to explore the concept carefully because it has always been clear that he saw a new *jahiliyya* in which Nasser and all the Arab modernists attempted to overwhelm Muslims and their faith. This *time of ignorance* required a new *jihad*. For liberated Egypt and its new government this was too much. Sayyid Qutb was hanged at dawn on 29 August 1966. For some he was a martyr (*shahid*), but to the authorities at Al-Azhar as-Sharif he was a heretic (*munharif*). Muhammad Qutb was released from an Egyptian jail in 1972 and settled in Saudi Arabia where he taught at Mecca's Umm al-Qura University and published many new editions of his brother Sayyid's books. Muhammad Qutb's best-known book since 11 September 2001 is entitled *Jahiliyya in the Twenty-First Century*. It cannot be a surprise to hear that those hoping to bring external *jihad* to the Islamic world – propagating faith 'by sword-and-book' – are now known as *qutbists*.

In October 2004 the BBC showed *The Power of Nightmares* by Adam Curtis, a rare presentation of Sayyid Qutb, pop-eyed and staring angrily at his interrogators. The programme portrays Qutb as a man obsessively reacting against American vulgarity, sexuality and materialism. But the essential message of this programme was that Bush and Blair no longer promise to fulfil the dreams and needs of their people but compulsively plan to protect their nations from the nightmares of terrorism. In a world of polarities and differences the alternative to Sayyid Qutb presented in *The Power of Nightmares* is American neo-conservatism, represented by Professor Leo Strauss of Chicago and his many disciples – Francis Fukuyama (*The End of History*), Samuel Huntington (*The Clash of Civilisations*), Rumsfeld, Cheyney and others. The neo-conservative message is not far from Qutb's but Strauss believed that the way to unite America was to create the myth of a country with a unique destiny to fight evil all over the world, even when the evil is imaginary. Since the 'coalition' invasion of Iraq there is a now a strong suggestion that we are all living in a climate of politically induced fear and threat. Paranoia is the principal weapon. We are called to see enemies everywhere. There are serious debates amongst Christians and Muslims about every kind of violence, especially bombing and beheading: *The Power of Nightmares* is sufficiently reliable to awaken our moral senses. The overwhelming majority of people being killed by both Islamic terrorists and coalition aerial bombardment are women and children.

In his words and through his example Sayyid Qutb lives on.

LISTENING TO ISLAM

with

Sayyid Qutb

"There is a secure rule in our approach to the Qur'an. We must come within reach of all the Quranic statements in order to derive our concepts and formulate our ideas from them. What the Qur'an says is absolute: *it is as it is*.

The Qur'an comes from God, the Supreme. So the Qur'an is binding upon us in the sense that whatever it states is the foundation of our otherwise very 'rational' concepts. Human reason is not the judge of what the Qur'an says. The Qur'an alone is the authority."

Sayyid Qutb, *In the Shade of the Qur'an*

Sayyid Qutb,
> an educationalist and
>   major Arabic literary commentator,

has made a positive contribution to Quranic studies because of what Kenneth Cragg calls his "literary cherishing of the Qur'an": his "deep emotion is, of course, utterly authentic and . . . played a great part in his exegesis." As a key ideologue of the Muslim Brotherhood, espousing violence and the overthrow of the Egyptian government in the 1950s and '60s, Qutb's contribution to Islam for the last half-century has been negative, but his personal passion is entirely positive, as we read in one of his earliest works, *Social Justice in Islam* (*Al'Adala al-Ijtima'iyya fi'l-Islam*):

> "*Islam offers mankind a perfectly integrated and exemplary system, the like of which the earth has not known either before the coming of Islam or since.*

> "*Islam does not seek, and has never sought, to copy any system whatsoever or to allow any sort of link or similarity between itself and others. It has chosen its own particular and exclusive path. Islam has offered to humanity a wholly integrated treatment of all human issues.*"

At the beginning of the twenty-first century it is essential to listen to Sayyid Qutb because of his deep personal devotion to God through the Qur'an, his hatred of all apparently 'secular' Muslim societies, and his contempt for those living in unIslamic nations whilst still calling themselves Muslims. His affirmations are not unlike those of a 'born again' Evangelical Protestant, for when he joined the Muslim Brotherhood he said "I was born in 1951". Bound to a religious text, Qutb is hardly different from the American Bible Belt Fundamentalist. In 1970, some years after his death, Qutb's personal testimony concerning the centrality of the Qur'an appeared in the Lebanon. He affirmed that he had never found himself in need of "anything but the Qur'an . . . anything else seems inadequate compared with anything we find in this amazing Qur'an." Piety did not assuage his anger with secularism. Perhaps more than most of his contemporaries, Qutb needed to find a path through the Holy Book itself which would provide some means of overcoming the ignorance of nominal Muslims and of other societies that have no place for God. Fundamentalists in all religions relate to their sacred text through that which they impose upon it.

It is clear that the fundamental literary and personal doctrine of the Qur'an, within Qutb's preview, is *I'jaz*: the incomparability of the Qur'an, its eloquence, poetic quality, matchlessness and the miraculous excellence of its language. Its divine source and authority attest all of these attributes. Being in Arabic is being the Qur'an, and there is no 'real' translation. A passion for the literary and aesthetic quality of the Qur'an is quite obvious to the reader of Qutb's multi-volume commentary 'In the Shade of the Qur'an' (*Fi Zilal al-Qur'an*). Before the time of his political terrorism, Qutb was most concerned with, and highly sensitive to, the quality of Quranic language. During his time as *litterateur* Qutb was one of many thinkers, Muslim and secular who argued – as Leonard Binder, a major researcher of Qutb's work indicates – that "in the field of religion as in the communicative sciences generally it is consciousness and not knowledge upon which truth, or reality, or Being, is to be grounded. In particular, Qutb is to be associated with those who have argued or intimated that the aesthetic is the appropriate form of discourse on religious, social and historical matters." But even in his earliest works Qutb is not referring to the role of the prophet, artist or interpreter when speaking of the matchless Qur'an. The Artist is God. Most powerfully, yet in English translation, when commentating upon *Surah 96 Al-'Alaq*, Sayyid Qutb's affirmation of faith in Quranic *I'jaz* retains the necessary force when he refers directly to the event of revelation, as God speaks to his prophet:

> 'The true nature of this event is that God . . . out of his benevolence, has turned to that creation of His called man . . . The period that followed the event was twenty-three years of direct contact between the human race and the Supreme Society.'

As Cragg tells us in *The Mind of the Qur'an*, "To admit human elements in the structure of the Qur'an is impossible to Islamic religion."

Qutb's massive commentary on Islam's holy book, which is

available in clear and coherent English, requires and deserves careful study. An illustration of the quality of 'In the Shade of the Qur'an' (*Fi Zilal al-Qur'an*) can be found in his beautiful exposition of the ninety-sixth chapter (*surah*) of the Qur'an.

Surah 96
Al-'Alaq (The Clot of Congealed Blood).

Read! (or Proclaim), in the name of your Lord and Cherisher,
Who created Created man, out of a (mere) clot of congealed blood:
Proclaim! And your Lord is Most Bountiful,
He who taught (the use of) the Pen,
– Taught man that which he did not know.
Nay, but man transgresses all bounds, in that he looks upon himself
    as self-sufficient.
Verily, to your Lord is the return (of all).

(Abdullah Yusuf Ali, 1934)

(*Al-Alaq*: trans. 'The Germ Cell' [Muhammad Asad]; 'The Sperm Cell' [Kenneth Cragg]; 'The Clinging Form' [M. A. S. Abdel Haleem]).

According to classical Islamic scholarship, it is generally agreed that *Surah 96* 'The Clinging Form' (Haleem) was the first Quranic revelation, mediated by the Archangel Gabriel and sent down (*tanzil*) into the mind and upon the lips of Muhammad. The revelation took place outside the prophet's cave on Mount Hira, when Muhammad was about forty years of age. This earliest disclosure of the Qur'an occurred on a night that became the most important in the Islamic month of Ramadan. It was *Lailat al-Qadr*, the Night of Power, described by Qutb as "the greatest and most significant event the universe has ever witnessed. It is the event which explains most clearly how human life benefits by God's planning, management and organisation." *Surah 96 Al-'Alaq* is central to the religious experience of Sayyid Qutb, as it is to most Muslims and as it must be for any Christians engaged in interfaith dialogue. Qutb's comments are apt:

> *"I reflected for a while upon this event. We have all read it many times*
> *. . . but we either read it casually, or give it little thought, and go on*

35

with our reading. Yet this is an event that has immense significance. It is an event which has an important bearing on the life of humanity . . . it is no exaggeration to describe this event as the greatest in the long history of human existence.

"The true nature of this is event is that God has turned to man, who takes his abode in a hardly visible corner of the universe, the name of which is Earth . . . God has honoured this species by choosing one of its number (Muhammad) to be the recipient of his light and wisdom.

"This is something infinitely great. Some aspects of its greatness become apparent when man tries . . . to perceive the essential qualities of God: absolute power, freedom from all limitations and everlastingness; and when he reflects . . . on the basic qualities of God's servants who are subject to certain limitations of power and life duration."

This is Sayyid Qutb at his most passionate – literary and even mystical. But even this exposition ends with a personal attack upon Gamal 'Abd al-Nasser and the new Republican Government. He was almost certainly writing in the Tora prison:

"The surah . . . refers to every obedient believer calling men to follow the path of God and to every tyrant who forbids prayer, threatens the believers and acts arrogantly."

Qutb's exposition of Islam in this important commentary most often refers to the innermost being of the Muslim believer, inviting one who believes to practice and realise the faith for themselves. But even in his interpretation of 'The Germ Cell' (Asad: *Surah* 96), it is quite clear that the groundwork is already being laid for political terrorism, no doubt beginning with the Brotherhood's attempt upon President Nasser's life in 26 October 1954:

"Do not obey this tyrant who tries to stop you from offering your devotion and conveying your message . . . leave him to the guards of hell who are sure to mete out to him what he deserves."

Sadly, in Qutb's complete overview of the Qur'an – and in what he perceived as the 1950s period of Egyptian national apostasy – revolutionary violence became a necessity. For his latest disciples in the twenty-first century there was a fundamental continuity between the Brotherhood's attempt on Nasser's life and the slaughter of children in Beslan on 3 September 2004. Vladimir Putin is perceived by some as an Eastern European Nasser, dominating Muslims in the Caucasus. Russian copies of Qutb's works and copies of the authentic Arabic Qur'an lay on the floors of the school in North Ossetia. Vladimir Khodov, a Russian Orthodox convert to Islam, was one of the terrorists involved in the massacre and he was a *qutbist*. Sayyid Qutb – the exegete who quite justifiably extolled the lyrical virtues of the Qur'an – became the poet of annihilation.

Jahiliyya is a central concept in the writing of Sayyid Qutb, receiving its clearest and most aggressive exposition in *Ma'alim 'ala-l-Tariq* (translated variously as *Signposts on the Way* or as *Milestones*). *Jahiliyya* is the *time of ignorance*. It refers to the ignorance of pagan, pre-Islamic Arabia. It has been used to denote periods of abuse in Islamic history. For Qutb, the Muslim Brotherhood in the 1950s and '60s struggle against Nasser vigorously applied it to the Egyptian administration. Now, twenty-first century Islamic activists acknowledge the present *jahiliyya* and fight for its defeat. They are consequently called upon to attack nominal and heretical Muslims and the unbelieving enemy. *Jahiliyya* is an important concept in the modern Islamic lexicon.

The term *neojahiliyya* is a neologism, widely employed in recent years. But we should adhere to Qutb's *Jahiliyya*, the *time of ignorance* not only in the seventh, twelfth and twentieth centuries but also now in the twenty-first. It is not merely the ignorance of the past but it is the *time of ignorance* that prevails anywhere in the Muslim world and beyond. The *Jahiliyya* proclaimed by *qutbists* must be reversed in the Middle East, Indonesia, the Caucasus or anywhere claiming to be Islamic: if it is not then the effect upon Islam could be disastrous.

Qutb taught that a truly Islamic society is not only one where people simply call themselves Muslims. It must be a society where Islamic Law (*shariah*) has a proper status: where prayers (*salat*), fasting (*saum*), pilgrimage (*hajj*), the confession of faith (*shahadah*) and appropriate charity (*zakat*) are all practised. *Jahiliyya* ends when the pillars of Islam are upheld everywhere. For Qutb and all who have learnt from him, Islamic society must not be one in which people follow their own version of Islam, and even call it 'progressive Islam': it must stand in the *shariah* and within the five pillars. The world of *Jahiliyya* appears in a variety of forms, but any *time of ignorance* is in defiance of God's guidance through the Qur'an. In his commentary on *Surah 109 Al-Kafirun* ('Those Who Deny the Truth.' Asad) Qutb writes of his native Egypt and the modern world as places of decadence, contaminated with Western influences and dominated by 'liberal Muslims' who were reproducing *the time of ignorance*:

> *"Jahiliyya and Islam are two totally different entities, separated by a wide gulf. The only way to bridge that gulf is for Jahiliyya to liquidate itself completely and substitute for all its law, values, standards and concepts their Islamic counterpart . . . until the people of Jahiliyya embrace Islam completely: no intermingling, nor half measures or conciliation is permissible . . . the chief characteristic of a person who calls on others to adopt Islam is the clarity of this fact within himself and his solemn conviction of being radically different from those who do not share his outlook. They have their religion. He has his. His task is to change their standpoint so that they may follow his path without compromise."*

Qutb's interpretation of *Jahiliyya* has retained its effectiveness. Radicals have employed Qutb's clever verbal coinage recently in Iraq. They speak of the *Jahiliyya* of the interim national government in Baghdad. The acting premier, Iyad Allawi is identified by fundamentalist clerics as "a dog directed by Americans and injected by them with the rabies virus." He is "living in a time of ignorance" *(Jahiliyya)*. But the term has been more widely used in Afghanistan, Chechnya, Indonesia, Jordan, Syria and Egypt; and perhaps most dogmatically against the *Royal House of Saud* in Saudi Arabia. It is generally believed that Qutb's *Signposts/Milestones/Ma'alim 'ala-l-Tariq*, which has been translated into more than sixty languages, has become the operations manual for terrorist cells in all these countries.

But caution is required from any Western observer, for the 'sacred patriotism' of the White House is even more terrifying. In 2004, there is no separation of church and state in the United States, despite the past agonising of George Washington, Thomas Jefferson and Abraham Lincoln. The reader may examine the next few lines, asking what the source, or sources, of this paragraph might be:

"Any system in which the final decisions are referred to human beings, and in which the sources of all authority are human, deifies human beings by appointing others than God as lords over men . . . to proclaim the authority and sovereignty of God means to eliminate all human kingship and to announce the rule of the Sustainer of the universe over the entire Earth . . . to establish God's rule means that His laws be enforced and that the final decision in all affairs be according to these laws."

Although the reader's answer might reasonably be Bush/Cheney/Rumsfeld, as suggested by David Hare's play *Stuff Happens*, the correct answer is Sayyid Qutb in *Milestones/Signposts*. No single 'religion' carries the responsibility for terrorist campaigns, ethnic-cleansing, inter-communal violence and even war. Faith-driven violence is everywhere.

Sayyid Qutb's theological denunciations of Coptic and Nestorian Christianity are comparatively calm. They occur in his Quranic commentaries on *Surah 98 Al-Bayyinah* ('The Clear Evidence', Ali); *Surah 109 Al-Kafirun* ('The Disbelievers'. Haleem); and *Surah 112 Al-Ikhlas* ('Purity of Faith', Ali). The list is far from exhaustive.

It is the famous *sword-verse* of the Qur'an (*Surah 9.5*), which instructs Muslims to 'kill the *mushrikun* (unbelievers) wherever you find them', that is the most widely cited example of Islam's aggressive commands. It is the *sword-verse* that remains a significant part of Coptic Christian fears for their Egyptian Muslim compatriots, most especially the Muslim Brotherhood (*al-Ikhwan al-Muslimin*).

Any reader of Sayyid Qutb, in any language, must understand the difference between *In the Shade of the Qur'an* and the equally, if not more, influential *Signposts/Milestones*. *In the Shade* may be read by anyone concerned with inter-faith dialogue who wishes to study the Qur'an, and even Christian readers will sympathise with the occasional outburst from Qutb given that he wrote most of this commentary in prison. *Signposts* is another matter. The revolutionary Muslim 'Sister' Zaynab al-Ghazali, commenting on Qutb's execution in 1966, said, "If you want to know why Sayyid Qutb was sentenced to death read *Signposts*." It is in this book that Qutb tells the reader how the Qur'an should be approached "as a soldier on the battlefield reads his daily bulletin so that he knows what is to be done." It is often stated that Qutb taught his disciples the practice of taking isolated passages from scripture out of context, so that they might be used as mantras or talismans rather than as sources of moral and spiritual guidance. *Proof-texts* are common in biblical Fundamentalism. In 1 Corinthians 14.35 (NRSV) we may read, "For it is shameful for a woman to speak in church." Proof sufficient for the Christian Fundamentalist that the ordination of women is an error. *Surah 9 At-Tawbah, aya* 5 in the Qur'an gives an instruction to "fight and slay the Pagans where you find them, and seize them, beleaguer them, and lie in wait for them" (Ali). Any comparable Quranic fundamentalists might easily think in the same literalist manner. For the *qutbist*, this *sword-verse* is to be interpreted as an instructional manual in military action, rather than as an inward or mystical directive. In his important translation and commentary *The Message of the Qur'an*, Muhammad Asad firmly states that 'every verse of the Qur'an must be read and interpreted against the background of the Qur'an as a whole.' Sayyid Qutb could not agree, for he shaped the thinking of his contemporaries and of the majority of present militant Islamic cells. In a moment of crisis a single verse is allowed to outweigh the Qur'an.

The movements, cadres and cells based upon Qutb's hopes for an Islamic utopia have more power in the twenty-first century than at most other times in Muslim history. But these groups need to be understood, and this is especially true of their connection with *Signposts*, which occupies a central place in the lives and thoughts of many modern Muslim extremists. Sayyid Qutb described these cells as a 'vanguard' destined to destroy and replace Nasser's government with an Islamic state:

> "How to initiate the revival of Islam? A vanguard must set out with this determination and then keep going, marching through the vast ocean of Jahiliyya, which encompasses the entire world. During its course, this vanguard, while distancing itself somewhat aloof from this all-encompassing Jahiliyya should also retain contacts with it. The Muslims in this vanguard must know the landmarks and the milestones on the road to this goal so that they would know the starting point as well as the nature, the responsibilities, and the ultimate purpose of this long journey. Not only this, but

they ought to be aware of their position vis-à-vis *this Jahiliyya which has struck its stakes throughout the earth. They must know when to cooperate with others and when to separate from them; what characteristics and qualities they should cultivate; and with what characteristics and qualities the Jahiliyya, immediately surrounding them, is armed; how to address the people of Jahiliyya in the language of Islam; what topics and problems to discuss with them; and where and how to obtain guidance in all these matters . . . I have written Signposts for this vanguard, which I consider to be a waiting reality about to be materialised."*

It is evident that Qutb's description of this *vanguard* has powerfully influenced radical Islam. *Al-Qaeda* may be a convenient label to apply to one form of Islamic militancy influenced by Qutb, but in reality one should refer to a wide-ranging strain of violent activists. Jason Burke, in his *Al-Qaeda. The True Story of Radical Islam* (2004), has shown that *al-Qaeda* in the twenty-first century has become the most extensive and dangerous convergence of international Quranic fundamentalists and Islamic terrorists. The events of 11 September 2001 were a tragedy that will extend into the foreseeable future. Osama bin Laden, born in Saudi Arabia in 1957, has become the pre-eminent figure in contemporary Islamic militancy. He benefits from as much media coverage as Bush or Blair. He has met with substantial success, but he is not a lone reader of Sayyid Qutb. (The Title *Al-Qaeda* could have a range of meanings from base, camp, home, rule, model or even 'vanguard' once again. The designation has real emotional power but it is not perceived as an organisation: it is a summons and − perhaps for many disadvantaged young Muslims − a vocation). Gilles Kepel describes *Signposts/Milestones* as "the royal road to the ideology of the Islamicist movement of the seventies" and as a "manifesto for radical Islamism." The influence of the text must now be extended into the next four decades for it would appear that Qutb's 'vanguard' has already materialised.

Signposts/Milestones is frequently described as the Islamic revolutionary's equivalent of the Soviet classic *What Is To Be Done?* or Communist China's *Little Red Book*. Lenin's volume is, in fact, much shorter than *Ma'alim 'ala-l-Tariq*, and *The Thoughts of Chairman Mao* a little longer than Sayyid Qutb's text, but in most English language versions of *Signposts/Milestones* the opening pages are authoritative: "Humanity today stands on the brink of the abyss." In Qutb's view, we might have lived and developed harmoniously but we are living in a sphere without values. The Western world has no adequate democracy and the dominant but failing economic systems are both socialism and capitalism. Even in his commentary on *Surah 103 Al-'Asr.* ('The Declining Day'. Haleem). Qutb aggressively attacks the evolutionist Charles Darwin, the psychologist Sigmund Freud and the political philosopher Karl Marx, whose major works he describes as "among the most horrid disasters human nature has encountered . . . They teach mankind that all abasement and downright animalism are natural phenomena with which we should be familiar and of which we need not be ashamed." In relation to evolutionary science, psychology and politics, Qutb as commentator reinforces his absolute, traditionalist teaching: "the Qur'an comes from God alone." In his further exegesis of *Surah 105 Al-Fil* ('The Elephant'; shared title in all translations):

> "Although human reason is, in essence an absolute force, not subject to, or limited by, individual experiences or events, it is, after all, confined to human existence . . . human reason is not the arbiter of what the Qur'an states."

In *Ma'alim 'ala-l-Tariq* (Signposts/Milestones) we hear that "Mankind needs a new direction!" Individualist and collectivist ideologies have both failed. Now it is the turn of Islam, of the *umma* (the community of believers) and not the *watan* (the nation), to realise the true aims of human life. The *umma* are those whose intellectual, social, existential, political and moral lives are based upon Islam alone: only those who are governed by the law of God have any future.

> "Today, the entire world lives in the state of ignorance (Jahiliyya), opposing God's rule on earth. To oppose the rule of God by accepting any other form of sovereignty is to be the enemy of faithful Muslims. When Muslim countries conquer the world then the umma must come to life."

It is clear that the introductory pages of *Signposts* do indeed offer not only an analysis of contemporary society but also a guide for the Islamic cadres. It is a manifesto – perhaps closer to Marx and

Engels than Lenin or Mao – but its message, delivered in sharp slogans, is always clear: 'Islam is the solution to the problems of humanity.' The ever-recurring revolutionary concept, much against the perception of most modern Muslims, is that *a state of ignorance*, whether historical or contemporary, continues to exist throughout the world and must be recreated:

> *"Any society that is not Muslim is Jahiliyya, as is any society anywhere in which something other than God alone is worshipped . . . Therefore, we must include in this category all the societies that now exist on earth."*

The societies discussed by Qutb include Communist traditions that deny God, and in which the object of worship is the political party, or other communities that are dominated by physical necessity and greed: "human needs are reduced to those of animals." *Jahiliyya* must include those societies where sovereignty is exercised in the name of the people or the political party and not in the name of God. Christian and Jewish societies may be the same, but the worst are those that describe themselves as Muslim but exercise sovereignty other than the sovereignty of God alone:

> *"Humanity today is living in a large brothel! One has only to glance at its press, films, fashion shows, beauty contests, ballrooms, wine bars, and broadcasting stations! Or observe its mad lust for naked flesh, provocative postures, and sick suggestive statements in literature, the arts and the mass media! And add to all this the system of usury which fuels man's voracity for money and engenders vile methods for its accumulation and investment, in addition to fraud, trickery, and blackmail dressed up in the garb of law."*

Sayyid Qutb clearly understood that the way forward was not through theological discourse or religious proclamation. The cadres of the Muslim Brotherhood in the Nasser period were no different from those who operated in New York and other places. It is Qutb who tells us that it would be foolish to limit any process of Islamic radicalism to words alone:

> *"To establish the reign of God on earth and eliminate the reign of man, to take power out of the hands of those of God's worshippers who have usurped it and to return it to God alone, to confer authority upon divine law alone and to eliminate the laws created by man . . . all this will not be done through sermons and discourses.*

"Those who have usurped the power of God on earth and made His worshippers their slaves will not be dispossessed by means of word alone, otherwise the task of his messenger would be far more easily done."

Fortunately, inter-faith dialogue has not died. But in this summary discussion of Sayyid Qutb and his teaching it is essential for the non-Muslim commentator to note that Islamic Orthodoxy has roundly condemned Sayyid Qutb, not only at the time when he wrote *Signposts/Milestones* but also in this twenty-first century when he is identified with terrorism. In response to the direction of Sheikh Hasan Ma'Mun the Grand Sheikh of al-Azhar as-Sharif, another Muslim cleric, Sheikh Muhammad 'Abd al-Latif al-Sibki, the president of the university's *fatwa* commission at that time, produced a detailed commentary upon Qutb's revolutionary manifesto. The Sheikh condemned the unorthodox *Ma'alim 'ala-l-Tariq* for its inflammatory style, blasphemy and sectarianism:

"Although in style Signposts is packed with verses from the Qur'an and references to Islamic history, in reality it is no more than the style of the saboteur, of the sort of activist who, in any society, Muslim or other, mixes truth and lies so that dissimulation is possible. Signposts was written with the intention of deluding the simple-minded and turning them into fanatics and blind assassins . . . the message of the so-called Muslim Brotherhood is no more than a plot against the national revolution, under the semblance of religious fervour . . . Those who act to circulate this book . . . are seeking to cause Egypt to degenerate and to inflict calamities upon it."

This firm judgement from the centre of Islamic Orthodoxy needs to be carefully weighed, but it is certainly clear that Sayyid Qutb's *Signposts* provided the starting blocks for the running track upon which the militants of Islamic Fundamentalism would travel, for he certainly believed that it was only through an authentic Islamic way of life that men could be freed from the servitude of some men to others, devoting themselves "to the worship of God alone, deriving guidance from Him alone, and bowing before Him alone."

Christian or agnostic analysts of the works of Sayyid Qutb should exercise great caution in any critical assessment of this important ideologue of the Muslim Brotherhood. Qutb certainly served the Egyptian-based brotherhood for several years. That he was its most important literary figure is beyond question. The two windows on his literary world must be looked through: the sense of Quranic wonder and the politics. A similar prudence should be exercised when examining modern Islamic terrorist groups, even though it is clear that Qutb's politics inspired most of them. The West – Christian or secular – must also look at itself. Neo-conservative politics and allied Christian fundamentalist religion in the United States define a society that is not a democracy but a plutocracy. The bombing of civilians – of Iraqi women and children – is an incalculable evil. In Islamic lands terrorism and anarchy have never achieved theocracy. Dialogue is possible, but any dialogue between Islam and Christianity would be a meaningless notion in the absence of more than one Muslim or Christian perspective.

Ironically, the verse (*aya*, sign) in the Qur'an most quoted in inter-faith dialogue is from a Medinan *sura* (Qur'an 2.256. *Al-Baqarah.*) 'The Cow' is the longest chapter in the Qur'an, but this solitary verse might just as easily have been delivered in Mecca during the time of persecution. It is interesting that the word *din* may be translated as 'religion' or 'faith, the former usually referring to the institutions and the latter expressing mankind's attitude towards the object of his worship. In a number of Muslim commentaries it is noted that any attempt to coerce a non-believer into accepting the faith of Islam is a grave sin: a theological opinion which disposes of the common myth that Islam places before unbelievers the alternatives of conversion or the sword. It is unlikely that Sayyid Qutb would have agreed.

Qur'an 2.256. *Al-Baqarah*, 'The Cow' (Asad & Haleem)

'*Let there be no compulsion in religion.*' (Ali)
'*There shall be no coercion in matters of faith.*' (Asad)
'*There is no place for compulsion in religion.*' (Cragg)
'*There is no compulsion in religion.*' (Haleem)

SOURCES FOR THE STUDY OF SAYYID QUTB

Geneive Abdo, *No God But God*, OUP, Oxford 2000.
Moustafa Ahmed, *Egypt in the 20th Century. Chronology of Major Events*, Megazette Press, London 2003.

Abdullah Yusuf Ali, *The Qur'an Translation*, TTQ Inc., New York 1995.

Tariq Ali, *The Clash of Fundamentalisms. Crusades, Jihads and Modernity*, Verso, London 2002.

Muhammad Asad, *The Message of the Qur'an*, Dar Al-Andalus Ltd., Gibraltar 1980.

Leonard Binder, *Islamic Liberalism: A Critique of Development Ideologies*, University of Chicago Press, Illinois, 1988.

Jason Burke, *Al-Qaeda. The True Story of Radical Islam*, Penguin, London 2004.

Ian Buruma & Avishai Margalit, *Occidentalism. A Short History of Anti-Westernism*, Atlantic Books, London 2004.

Michael Cook, *The Koran, A Very Short Introduction*, OUP, Oxford 2000.

Kenneth Cragg, *The Pen and The Faith. Eight Modern Muslim Writers and the Qur'an*, George Allen and Unwin, London 1985.

Mark Juergensmeyer, *Terror in the Mind of God. The Global Rise of Religious Violence*, University of California Press, Berkeley 2000.

Gilles Kepel, *The Prophet & Pharaoh. Muslim Extremism in Egypt*, Al Saqi Books, London 1985.

——, *The War for Muslim Minds*, Harvard University Press, Massachusetts 2004.

Oliver McTernan, *Violence in God's Name. Religion in an Age of Conflict*, Darton, Longman and Todd, London 2003.

Malise Ruthven, *Islam, A Very Short Introduction*, OUP, Oxford 1997.

——, *A Fury For God: The Islamist Attack on America*. Granta, London 2002.

——, *Fundamentalism, The Search for Meaning*, OUP, Oxford 2004.

Sayyid Qutb, *In The Shade of The Qur'an (Fi Zilal al-Qur'an)*, 18 vols in English from 30 vols in Arabic. The Islamic Foundation. Leicestershire, UK 2004/1425.

——, *Milestones. 'Signposts on the Way' (Ma'alim 'ala-l-Tariq)* (Trans. Ahmad Zaki, Indianapolis, n.d.

Available online: <http://www.youngmuslims.ca/online_library/books/milestones/index.htm>; <http://gemsofislamism. tripod.com/milestones. html>

Sayyid Qutb, *Milestones*. American Trust Publications, CA, n.d. anonymous translation.

Sayyid Qutb, *This Religion of Islam (Hadha 'd-Din)*, Al-Manar Press, California 1967.

KENNETH CRAGG

Biographical Outline

"Footwear has the lowly function of perpetually conditioning the tread of the owner's feet. It interposes between him and all terrain. It mediates to him the vicissitudes of his pathway. Our Christian sandals, in a figure, brought us to the mosque door as careful students."

Kenneth Cragg, *Sandals at the Mosque*

ALBERT KENNETH CRAGG WAS BORN IN BLACKPOOL,
LANCASHIRE ON 8 MARCH 1913.

His first Christian name came from his father who was a local merchant, though his parents always called him Kenneth. At the time of writing he is in his ninety-first year and bursting with intellectual energy. Hospitality is a key word for all his friends and admirers. His kindness and generosity are legendary.

The biography of Kenneth Cragg is compelling and disturbing. His life is an affirmation of faith but not of institutional religion. Cragg has experienced three bitter ecclesiastical redundancies in his long life but his Christian stoicism is legendary: "It is the mystery of yourselves that you receive." His autobiographical outline, *Faith and Life Negotiate. A Christian Story-Study* (1994), is not an 'exercise in egoism' but a quest of faith's themes within individual life. It is a book that repays study.

Dr. Cragg's Christian life began in Christ Church Blackpool, a "nursery for evangelical loyalty", with a "warm and simple form of Anglicanism", devoted to the Book of Common Prayer and the proclamation of the Gospel. He won a scholarship to Blackpool Grammar School, and that school joined his parish church as the second governing influence in his teenage life. The class preparing for matriculation included a number of Jewish scholars though the most famous pupil at the Grammar School, who was three years senior to Cragg, was Alistair Cooke, the famous author of the BBC's *Letter from America*. Cooke graduated from Jesus College, Cambridge and Cragg from Jesus College, Oxford (BA '34: MA '38). Cragg went on to read Theology at Tyndale Hall, Bristol (Trinity College), and was ordained Deacon in 1936 and Priest in 1937, serving as a Curate in Chester Diocese from 1936 to '39.

During his curacy Kenneth fell in love with Melita Arnold. They were engaged in 1938. But this was a most significant, even dramatic, moment in their lives, because he was one of a minority of Anglicans at the time who was placing Arabic and Islam firmly on this couple's map. He was bound for Beirut, Lebanon in January 1939. She studied at Mount Hermon College in Streatham. They were to be separated for sixteen months. Melita finally travelled to

Beirut in May 1940, in the last civilian ship to cross the Mediterranean before Italy entered the sea war. Kenneth and Melita were married in All Saints' Beirut on 31 December 1940 by one of their heroes, Bishop George Francis Graham-Brown.

The Craggs served in Shimlan, Gaza and Beirut. Two sons were born in the Near East. At the American University in Beirut – an institution without reference to colour, nationality, race or religion – Kenneth and Melita established a residential hostel. He was appointed an Adjunct Professor in the university, teaching English and Philosophy. Their new hostel was named *St. Justin's House* after the great second century Palestinian Christian philosopher Justin Martyr.

In the summer of 1947 Kenneth Cragg returned to Oxford. He became Rector of Longworth for four years. Joy, their only daughter, died in her cot, only eight weeks of age, but a third son was born in their new parish. Kenneth was awarded an Oxford D.Phil. in 1951, after oral examination by the distinguished Arabist, Professor H. A. R. Gibb. The doctoral thesis was entitled: 'Islam in the Twentieth Century: The relevance of Christian theology and the relation of the Christian mission to its problems.' The unpublished work still rests in the Bodleian Library in Oxford. Dr. & Mrs. Cragg were due to return to the Middle East with their three boys, Arnold, John and Christopher, but the Church authorities refused Kenneth his Arabic Christian Islamic homecoming. With the pilgrimage to the Middle East closed, he travelled to the Hartford Seminary, Connecticut in 1951, to teach in the Islamic Department and edit the internationally famous quarterly *The Muslim World*. Granted a Rockefeller Travelling Fellowship in 1954, Kenneth flew to the Middle East, visiting Istanbul, Ankara, Aleppo, Damascus, Baghdad, Amman, Cairo, Tripoli, Tunis, Algiers, Fez and Tangier. It is known that his decades as a Christian scholar of Islam led him to make more than four hundred flights throughout the Muslim world, but that may be an underestimate. At Hartford, Kenneth Cragg produced his most important work in inter-faith studies, *The Call of the Minaret*.

In 1956 Kenneth Cragg returned to the Middle East, acting as Study Secretary for the Near East Council of Churches and Residentiary Canon of St. George's Cathedral Jerusalem. Most of his time was devoted to travel throughout the region. In addition to an enormous amount of academic work and travel in the Middle East, Cragg lectured in Pakistan, India, Ghana, Nigeria and Sierra Leone, engaging in vital dialogues with major Muslims scholars. The Council project ended in 1959.

Dr. Cragg served at St. Augustine's, the Central College of the Anglican Communion from 1959 to 1967. He was Warden from 1961 and appointed Honorary Canon at Canterbury Cathedral. The devastating closure of the college and Cragg's brutal expulsion as Warden is hardly surprising: the coldness and indifference of church authorities is well known. Even in the late 1960s — as in the '90s — 'churchmanship' was most probably an issue. It is most significant that Cragg's superior — when referring to the financial pressures at the Central College, and the complexity of comparative academic standards with clergy from all over the Anglican world — commented, "the product on offer was not worth the price tag attached".

The majority of Anglican clergy are notorious career-seekers. Cragg was a rare exception. But his ruling bishop was "strangely oblivious of what became to us in the dispersing". In 1967 Cragg left for Union Theological Seminary, New York. He was a Visiting Professor, and in 1968 filled an identical post in the Arabic and Theology Department at the University of Ibadan, Nigeria. In 1969 he worked as Bye-Fellow at Gonville and Caius, Cambridge. He was left waiting for a ministry. We should agree with Bishop Stephen Bayne that "Anglican history was littered with the wreckage of departed dreams". It is an understatement, but the corrupt often succeed.

Kenneth Cragg is an Anglican clergyman, but unlike most others. In his most memorable words concerning ordained service: "Ministry must be ever watchful of the bearing of its 'official' dignities, the rights of rites, on the inner secrecies of personal self-esteem, lest there be subtle usurpation at the very core of our servanthood." Cragg could employ his wit with a sharpness that would irritate some clergy: "Ministry does well not to be too often mitred, since the flames of Pentecost are not amenable to millinery . . . Jesus' only headgear in Jerusalem was the crown of thorns."

In 1970 Dr. Kenneth Cragg was consecrated to serve as an assistant Bishop in Jerusalem, operating across the whole Anglican Archbishopric from Morocco in the West to Iran in the East. It was planned that the Archdiocese be arabicised. Faced with all the anticipated changes within Middle Eastern Anglicanism a Western arabist was needed. In the immediate future only Arab bishops would be required. A new Province of Jerusalem and the Middle East was quickly prepared, in complete independence from Canterbury and with its own Synod. There would be a Palestinian bishop in Israel–Palestine, and a bishop for Cyprus and the Gulf. Egypt would have its own native diocesan bishop and Iran its native Persian. A Presiding Bishop could be elected from within the sprawling archdiocese. Cragg was, on this occasion, ready to embrace the Anglican changes in the Middle East. It was a sad departure for him, but quite unlike the appalling procedures in Beirut or Canterbury.

Cragg is the author of more than forty books and his internationally published academic papers are legion. He has been awarded doctorates of Divinity in Canada, the United States and England. He served as an assistant Bishop in Chichester (1973–78), whilst teaching as a Reader in Religious Studies at the University of Sussex. In Wakefield (1978–81) he acted as an advisor to teachers and clergy on Christian Islamic relations throughout West Yorkshire. The Craggs then moved on to Ascott-under-Wychwood in Oxfordshire in 1982.

Dr. Cragg was an assistant bishop in the Diocese of Oxford from 1982, Chevasse Lecturer at Oxford in 1983 and Sprigg Lecturer in Virginia in 1985. His beloved wife Melita died in 1989 and was buried at Ascott-under-Wychwood. Bishop Kenneth now lives close to Christchurch College in the city. It would be ludicrous to describe him as 'retired'. He remains an indefatigable traveller, author and lecturer. It is always possible to hear the true voice of Kenneth Cragg at his warmest and at his most vulnerable. In March 2002 at Cumberland Lodge in Windsor Great Park, in a post-September 11, 2001 world, we heard him once again:

> *"Faiths are always responsible for what their faithful have made of them. For these identify each other – which, as in an aphorism, is the paradox for which they are responsible. Being a 'world-Islam' or a 'world-Christianity' only makes us the more liable for magnanimity."*

LISTENING TO ISLAM

with

Kenneth Cragg

"Each of the monotheisms in the Middle East, guilty in their different ways of this bias for themselves against a right loyalty to God, has the onus on itself. Only out of the inner resources of these religions can the answer come. If humility avails, perhaps they can assist each other."

Kenneth Cragg, *The Arab Christian*

It is widely acknowledged that
extremist Christians – Catholic, Orthodox
and Protestant – as well as fundamentalist
Muslims – are suspicious of Kenneth Cragg.

A favourite story about the young academic of the American University in Beirut in the early 1940s, recounts his visit to student accommodation. He engaged both the Christian and Muslim students in a deeply reflective *tête-à-tête*. It was a time of immense kindness and conviviality. When Kenneth Cragg left the dormitory a Muslim student asked an Orthodox Christian, 'Is that Englishman a Muslim?' The compassion and flexibility of this impressive mind seem to have left more than a few believers, whether Christian or Muslim, to wonder about Kenneth's real allegiance.

Faced with the large library of Dr. Cragg's books it is necessary to focus upon a limited range of themes. But many of his most sensitive inter-faith publications will survive for decades. *The Call of the Minaret* (1956) and *Sandals at the Mosque* (1959) are possibly the favourite volumes of those – specialist or non-specialist – who need to know Islam through the mind and heart of this remarkable scholar. These two volumes express a central theme in Cragg's thought. He wishes to communicate with Islam, and with individual Muslims, through relationships rather than studied proclamation. Christopher Lamb, the foremost authority on Cragg's theology, has outlined the bishop's teaching in *A Faithful Presence* (2003). Lamb explains how Kenneth could not dismiss Islam as theologically shallow or inadequate, or by its role in any wider religious alliance against modern secularism. Cragg has retrieved a shared doctrine of Being and insisted upon the reciprocity of Christian–Islamic thinking about God and the world. Kenneth Cragg always focused upon the most positive aspect of Islamic life and thought, developing a form of mission that has the widest reference to shared thought and practice in the modern world. He is a messenger of peace between faiths not of hostile criticism or negative response.

In later life Kenneth was never free from the 'legacies of bitterness' in the Middle East. But too much space would be required here to examine two of his major works of the political religious frontier. *This Year in Jerusalem* (1982) examines the paradox of Zionism and its putative theology. *Palestine: The Prize and Price of Zion* (1997) has its own appeal concerning the fate of Christian-Palestine. Despite all the tragedies from May 1948 to the fiftieth anniversary of the foundation of the State of Israel, Cragg regards it as the supreme test of all the religions that they should kindle and transact the will to be forgiven and to forgive. Books about Israel Palestine are notoriously partisan and can hardly be expected to anticipate tomorrow's terrifying headlines, but here we can be confident of the integrity and balance of this author.

In his professional field of study, two themes have summarised Kenneth Cragg's life and thought more than any others. They are the *Qur'an* and the life of *Muhammad*. These subjects must be constantly linked to the modern world, as it is now known in politics and might be understood through Christian discipleship in ecumenism and interfaith dialogue. As a Christian Cragg has most often sought to sympathetically define the book and the biography as the subjects of deepest meaning in Muslim life as he has found it. He is a man of great learning and of greater faith, but he is also a person of the greatest modesty and humility.

We may turn briefly to Kenneth Cragg in the Qur'an and with Muhammad.

In *A Certain Sympathy of Scriptures: Biblical and Quranic* (2004) Cragg explores the Christian Scriptures in the twenty-first century and the Qur'an in the fifteenth Muslim century. There are three central topics: How the divine will is expressed for mankind, what the work of humankind is within creation, and how truth is revealed in the world. Dr. Cragg knows very well that there has been a long, "often polemical distrust of, or attack upon, the other's Scripture". But he hopes to overcome any denunciation from either side and to explore both the internal and external relationship between reader and text. "There are all the duties of scholarship between a reading historian and a reading theologian. For neither can be exegetes of that scriptured 'privilege' without the other". He hopes for a reading in "the neutral light of rational day", or at least in "the dim shadow of human despair". This deeply existential reading of Qur'an and Bible is not entirely unknown. But it is perhaps too optimistic to expect that many will search for what the truth of any scripture might have been for those who thought and wrote as they did. With notable Muslim exceptions, such a reading of the Qur'an is almost impossible. But Cragg is always deeply aware of the fact that classical Muslim exegetes, from every Islamic century, know that the Qur'an cannot be reduced to a single absolute meaning. There can be a plenitude of interpretations in which the Qur'an is listened to as both revelation and literary monument. There are Muslims everywhere who long to read the book in a multitude of different ways. In *Returning to Mount Hira: Islam in Contemporary Terms* (London 1994), Cragg quoted the modern Muslim scholar Muhsin Mahdi with approval:

> *"What the Qur'an meant for the original listeners and those around the Prophet, i.e. its original historical sense, does not exhaust its message to believers. For the Quranic message is in a sense ahistorical. It spoke to the first generations of Muslims, it spoke to every generation since them, it speaks to us and it will speak to the generations that succeed us."*

In both Scriptures – Christian and Muslim – a careful bonding between the history and the ahistorical are vital, and it is only the Fundamentalists in both traditions who would reject the ahistorical. We must always resist the temptation to identify all Muslim readers of the Qur'an with those like Osama bin Laden who have betrayed the Qur'an, or those in the White House who affirm a crude Biblical literalism. It is Kenneth Cragg, in his *Readings in the Qur'an* (1988, 2nd edition 1999), who is invariably at his best when he calls us to a right assessment of the text of the Qur'an we are reading:

> *" . . . to stay in a casual or only academic interest, to come to the Book simply out of curiosity, or for controversy, would be to forfeit the integrity it expects and requires. A right readership has need of a ready patience and a keen perception and, to inform these, the perspectives of hope. Wise readers will bring these steadily until the Book itself rewards them."*

Cragg always refused to associate himself with the impulse of those Christians who wished to express their unhappiness with the Qur'an by descending into condemnation and polemic. He was certain that a text that was obviously so precious and so final for such a large a segment of humankind demanded an open – even a generous – estimate: "awareness of its Arabic quality would have given pause to any easy dismissiveness", and in contrast to the narrow-minded majority in his own church he gave the Qur'an his attention and his love:

> *"The Qur'an's understanding of man in the world, of divine sovereignty and undergirding our creaturely hospitality in nature via the sacramental character of all our experience, and much else, drew me – like the fascination of calligraphy – into a long, positive reckoning with the Qur'an and a desire to get it more squarely into the consciousness of my fellow Christians and indeed of secular sceptics."*

Bishop Cragg has delivered us from the narrowness of vision that characterises so much of modern Christianity. His deep appreciation of Islamic faith, the prophet and the holy text survives because he lives with them in dialogue and creative tension. In *The Christ and the Faiths* (1986) his position is clear: "Theology in cross-reference is the only theology there is. There is no good faith that is not attentive". It is "by a steady attention to the questionings from which other faiths reach for their answers that the gospel makes its way, taking up those very questionings into the answer it holds for them through 'God in Christ reconciling the world'." To affirm the uniqueness of Christ is not to embrace exclusiveness. When the Johannine Jesus affirms, "I am the way, and the truth, and the life. No one comes to the Father except through me" (NRSV John 14.6), it is the 'how' of this coming that affects the thinking of all Christians who love Muhammad and the Qur'an. The two sentences are not an end; they are a beginning, reaching beyond the limitations of religion.

The Call of the Minaret (1956) has been in print for nearly half a century, and is by general consent Cragg's most persuasive work. It is certainly not too much to say that it is a masterpiece. In the first edition, the superb and educative third chapter carries a striking subtitle in Arabic letters, *wa-Muhammad rasul Allah*, 'and Muhammad is the messenger of God': in the second edition of this book, which remains in print, the title of chapter three has been reduced to an unadorned English heading, *Muhammad, the Apostle of God.* These thirty-three pages are of central importance for the Christian scholar and his readers. His acknowledgement of Arabic-language writers is affecting. One out of many examples comes from Muhammad Heikal, author of numerous important Islamic books, who writes of the Prophet:

> *"His is a power that can lift humankind to the heights of the spirit where life will be brotherhood and love and care for the knowledge of all that is in the world of existence, so that knowledge may illumine neighbourly concord and love, and that both may grow in human worth and excellence and bring us by their protection into the fullest peace."*

Dr. Cragg himself writes of Muhammad throughout his book and the reading is deep: we learn of 'the Sufi repossession of the mystical Muhammad', the modern social reformer's 'invocation of the iconoclast and the rebel', and of the contemporary philosopher, in the Islamic World and in the modern West, who appeals to 'the dynamic Muhammad.' In *Muhammad and the Christian* (1984), Cragg instructs his fellow Christians concerning a necessary appreciation of Islam's Prophet:

> *"In treating of Muhammad, he (the Christian) must know that he is moving within a sanctuary of soul-wonder, and not simply within a sequence of historical event. He is handling hearts' love."*

The Muhammad of Bishop Kenneth is close to the devotional image of so many Muslims: it is far from the preset, makeshift figure identified by many other religions. Christians ought to acknowledge the Prophet of Islam "for the sake of those same 'things of God', which move us to acknowledge him."

In *Muhammad in the Qur'an: the Task and the Text* (2001) we are constantly reminded of the connection between prophet and book. There is 'the central mystery of his inspiration, the language, the rhetoric, the eloquence' that belonged with the teacher and the manuscript. Muhammad "spoke the land's Arabic in its most expressive range and power . . . where the Scripture and the man cojoined, lies the central quest of all Quranic study, the whence and whither of a human agency in a divine summons".

The Muslim or Christian exegete who wishes to affirm Islamic Orthodoxy must speak of *Tanzil*, the sending down of the Qur'an into the mind and upon the lips of Muhammad. In the enigmatic delivery to the prophet the entire content of the Qur'an is *sent down*. Muhammad can recite to the letter the heavenly text *Umm al-Kitab* – the Mother of the Book – the eternal counterpart of the Qur'an, which resides in the presence of God alone. Muhammad's ministry of acceptance continued at intervals between the ages of forty and sixty-three. Not all Muslims are bound to the idea of Muhammad as the passive recipient of the text. Fazlur Rahman has explored the Qur'an to determine Muhammad as one who was an *active receiver* of the text. Rahman held that the divine guidance in the Qur'an operated through Muhammad in sacred collaboration and not simply with forceful imposition from above: 'there being no necessary contradiction between a divine granting and a human participating'. (This leading Pakistani exegete was dismissed as a heretic. But Dr. Rhaman continued his academic career in the West.) In reality, both Christian and Muslim scriptures must be subject to textual and theological criticism, though the task is extremely difficult.

There is no doctrine, no theological process, that describes the person of Muhammad. But just as there is the call to the *Christ-like* – expressed evangelically, 'my desire to be like Jesus' – so too *Muhammad-like* became the norm of true Muslim behaviour. Islamic community, like Christian church, was called to ascertain a pattern of behaviour. It is significant that the personal name 'Muhammad' occurs only four times in the Qur'an. He is known by his titles. He is *Al-Rasul*, the apostle or messenger of God, and sometimes as *Al-Nabi*, the seer or visionary. The fact that the titles displace the name can be seen as expressions of an individual, in the holy book, who is 'a personality wholly taken up into a religious destiny'. This must be true for all Muslims but it is especially significant for the devout Sufi for whom the example of Muhammad is of central spiritual – rather than intellectual or textual – significance. As Cragg notes, "Muhammad is the exemplar of the path. He exemplifies faith as an attitude rather than dictating it as a dogma." The witness of Muhammad has inspired, perhaps above all other sources, some of the greatest devotional literature in Islam, not necessarily through his name, but most certainly through his example.

If the orthodox Christian believer experiences any regret in a relationship with Islam it rests only in what Kenneth Cragg calls "the Caesar in Muhammad." The Meccan period in the early career of Muhammad was a time when the emerging faith was without power: one of Mecca's most beautiful traditions concerns the torture and persecution of the Negro slave *Bilal el-Habashi*, who became the first muezzin of Islam, calling the faithful to prayer. Islam in Mecca was persecuted. Islam in Medina became a power base. The political authority and military force in Medina is most eloquently presented in the substantial film *The Message* (Antony Quinn plays the main military leader Hamza: the prophet Muhammad is not shown on screen). Early Islam ends with the conquest of Mecca and the establishment of authority. Meccan persecution was liberated by Medina's martial strength.

In *Am I not your Lord? Human Meaning in Divine Question* (2003) Cragg argues for a "reverse abrogation": against the trend in Islamic tradition where the Medinan abrogates the Meccan he would like to see the Meccan abrogate the Medinan. In the bishop's view, "there can be no doubting the priority" of Mecca, where "Islam had no sanction but persuasion and a preached witness. The Medinan dimension of political and sovereign power, which it may have rightly coveted then, has no religious warrant now. It is to Mecca that the rite of pilgrimage goes, to Mecca that every mosque is pointed by its niche, to the preaching *Rasul* not the political figure that the *Shahada* witnesses." In sympathy with a Christian critic like Cragg, it is Fazlur Rahman who has said that his faith has to "reinvigorate the elements that are intrinsically Islamic", and by this he refers to the pacific beauty of Islam and not to the image of New York's descending towers and falling bodies – an unforgettable image of appalling human tragedy. No religion can speak lightly of the destructive force of religious institutions and surely the theologies of the Roman Catholic Inquisition, Protestant Fundamentalism, the Holocaust, the American Bible Belt and Serbian genocide all abrogate Calvary. If a strident Medina lives on, where is Mecca now?

Orthodox Muslims in every branch of their religion would seriously undermine any sanguine expectation of a "reverse abrogation", but Kenneth Cragg is at his most sympathetic when he examines late twentieth-century responses to Islam. It is within a believer's life that he discerns a Meccan recovery and a Medinan denial, which is both personal and historical. The biography is that of *Malcolm X* who became *Al-Hajji Malik al-Shabazz*. The two names embody Cragg's 'reverse abrogation'. 'Black Islam' had distorted a religion to serve racial hatred, and even religious hatred. Most Black Muslims directed their criticisms against Martin Luther King and his concepts of inter-racial, even inter-religious love. The man who had been *Malcolm X* undertook the pilgrimage to Mecca and there he discovered an Islam that was 'disciplined, zealot, assured and dignified'. When the rites of pilgrimage were performed a comprehensive inter-racialism that was 'tangible and palpable' was experienced. An assassin's bullet killed *Al-Hajji Malik al-Shabazz* in America: "He paid with his life for his radical progress into a hopeful, urgent, positive perception and practice of Islam." It may be true that a single biography cannot epitomise the inner life of a whole faith-system, but it is quite certain that faith may survive in any authentic living.

Kenneth Cragg is not unlike some Eastern spiritual fathers – a Russian *staretz*, Greek *geron* or Coptic *abba*. In the world of the spirit he walks the perilous tightrope between institutional religion and expressive faith. We should not speak of comparative religion but of faith encounter. He is possibly at his most radical in the book *Alive To God: Muslim and Christian Prayer* (1970) (cf. *Common Prayer: A Muslim–Christian Spiritual Anthology*, Oxford, 1999). This important text was carefully prepared during his time as a Bye-Fellow at Gonville and Caius, Cambridge, but only after decades of textual and inner preparation in Egypt, England, Nigeria and the United States. The subtitle is no doubt accurate in terms of the thought of the two faiths, though the book in fact includes great writers who could not be further from the two monotheistic faiths. Cragg embraces Bertolt Brecht the revolutionary German Communist author, Albert Camus the French Algerian writer, Alexei Gastev the Russian people's poet, UN Secretary General Dag Hammarskjöld and the Rumanian experimental dramatist Eugene Ionesco. The list could continue and includes more authors from Africa, Europe and the United States. In Cragg's preview: "The index of sources will suffice as proof of the range of our enlist-

ment. Close to twenty original languages and almost thirty countries, from the Java Sea to the Caribbean, are represented and many
of the well-nigh fourteen Muslim and twenty Christian centuries."

For Christian conservatives, who are most obviously armed and
on-the-march in the twenty-first century, the 23 Muslim sources
would be a problem. In the author's Egyptian Christian study
Among the Copts one of the bishops describes the God of Islam as
'Satan', and is rebuked by the Coptic patriarch for saying this. But
in the United States it is most frequently asserted that there is not
one God for Christians and Muslims. Cragg has a very different
perspective.

Cragg has a clear-eyed and critical view of his own faith and of
Islam. Christianity and Islam both deserve a positive appreciation
and some negative criticism. In *Alive to God* we have 99 pages of
devotion and an introductory essay of 55 pages. Cragg knows too
well that the monotheistic faiths are invariably in debate, but his
conclusions are always most helpful:

> "*There has, in truth, almost from the beginning, been long and loaded
> argument between Islam and Christianity. And the argument, controver-
> sially, entered into God, into conflict about his will, his nature, his justice,
> his knowledge, and his mercy. All of which are very urgent matters. But
> is there not another way before us of 'entering into God'?*"

When Eldridge Cleaver, the radical Black Panther leader,
discovers an Afro-American convert to Islam, he is most impressed
by this activist because his retreat from the "precipice of madness
created new room for others to turn about in, and I am caught up
in that tiny space". Cragg has always been aware of the "forces and
factors operating in all faith systems, interpreting their duties and
understanding their loyalties" in ways that are divergent. But he
embraces Cleaver's comment:

> "*'Room to turn in', however 'tiny', is the crux of the struggle and prayer
> is its only lodgement in the soul, its only tenure in the hating and hoping
> world.*"

And is there only one God, the Father of all? is the question posed
in Alan Ridout's mini-opera *Trial By Fire*, which concerns the
deaths by burning of a Franciscan Friar and a devout Sufi Imam

together in the same bonfire of the faiths. Any answer to the question is difficult but what Elridge Cleaver learned was that is possible to transform the negativity and hatred, which inspires so many belief systems, into a sense of a shared humanity. The dialogue lies in the transcendence and the sacrifice.

Cragg is ready to answer the question, *Do Christians and Muslims have the same God*? The answer can be 'Yes' and 'No'. But at the level of prayer that is present in his book *Alive to God* the answer must be *Yes*. Those central words that are affirmed, applied and asserted by Christians and Muslims concerning God frequently change, but both religions are bursting with mutual predicates and in their prayers there is the same Lord, who is the subject of "a large and loyal freedom". The two theologies may diverge, indeed they do, but both "relate alike to the one Lord". The Muslims and the Christians – and no doubt the scheduled sceptics and modernists included in *Alive to God* – worship the same Lord, in "worships informed by significantly similar, as well as sharply discordant, theology". Theology exists within and beyond language.

Being alive to the language of the Qur'an or to Christian scripture is no easy matter. Translation requires much more than technical skill. Commenting on Colin Turnbull's *The Lonely African*, Bishop Cragg studies the author's commentary upon the familiar pitfalls in the art of translation. Turnbull quotes a literal African language translation of the Prologue to St John's Gospel: "In the beginning was the Word, and the Word was with God and the Word was God." In the African language the sentence reads, "In the beginning there was a great argument, and the argument came with God, and the argument entered into God."

Cragg's lifelong engagement with the Qur'an could be seriously misunderstood if it were simply understood as an academic exercise. It is not, nor has it ever been. It was much more than a meeting of minds: "Dictionaries are . . . places of wonder . . . All words . . . have histories, and some of them extraordinary adventures" (*Call of the Minaret*). Cragg was constantly concerned about the use of language as a central place of exchange for "words are the highways of the traffic of ideas, sentiments, emotions, and relationships, and the work of the world is done by them." But in his meeting with the Qur'an there is also a spiritual dimension that remains of central importance for him. He quotes with approval the colourful phrase of Sir Edwyn Hoskyns (*Cambridge Sermons*, 1938): "Can we rescue a word, and discover a universe? Can we study a language, and awake to the Truth? Can we bury ourselves in a lexicon, and arise in the presence of God?" Cragg's answer in relation to Bible and Qur'an is a probing and sustaining 'Yes'.

The same sense of the weight of inner and external language survives in *Alive to God*. The word-heavy power of liturgical prayer can have strength in the liturgies of the churches and in the dignity of congregational *Salat* in the mosque, and these traditions of prayer will never become invalid or unsatisfying, but there are other searching demands upon us. Perhaps this is why Cragg gave space in his book of prayers to those powerful 'outsiders' and 'agnostics' whom we need "in alerting our language to what it must embrace". We cannot recoil from faith if we are believers, but we may salvage the witness of faith in our own time in a very different way. Institutional Christianity and Islam are not tranquil, and we must learn to be still. 'Underlying all speech there is a silence that is greater.'

Amidst the pressures of life "there is emerging a pattern of praying which is, as it were, simply meditative, not so much – as often hitherto – about the mysteries of faith, but rather about the tumults of the world". After the tragic events in New York in 2001, and all that followed, Cragg could not be more pertinent. In the existing violence of our times we must read our contemporary newspapers with "reflective responsibility", viewing the daily life of the world within the context of God's life. This deeply personal meditative prayer "wants to react in God and for God" when we understand "the plight and the passion" of the world. Such prayer may quietly supplant the weight of words, whilst knowing that "there is a corporate guilt about hunger, war, and tragedy, and a corporate menace in ignorance, enmity and violence". Cragg's understanding of prayer, which lies at the heart of all the prayers in *Alive to God*, cannot be appropriated by the words of the ages, however eloquent the poetry of liturgical prayer. For though "even wordless", such prayer means "a will to be a participant, a desire to atone, a purpose to care, a readiness to understand". This prayer is rooted – as it was in Kosovo and Palestine, in Bali and Beslan – in a sense of 'presence'. This unarticulated prayer of stillness and silence, which lives in the hearts and minds of those who believe, 'wants to be alive to God in being alert to mankind'.

Bishop Kenneth's latest book is *Semitism: The whence and the whither, 'How dear are your counsels'* (2005). The text bursts with the writer's scholarship, including careful examinations of modern politics relating to the present struggle in the Middle East. Cragg's long literary ministry has always been deeply conscious of the sense of difference within the Abrahamic faiths. But his protracted search for over half a century has been to find how history, theology and scripture in Christianity, Islam and Judaism might meet: "Religious faith is not a mere phenomenon about which sociology may debate as to its social role, nor are politics fit to make it a facilitator. Precisely in 'requiring truth in the inward parts', faith must stand above all these. By the same token it cannot well ignore them, still less despise them. History lays a long sanction on cultural and ethnic identities and faiths are long enmeshed within them." But the three faiths may soar above the institutional religions.

The *Semitism* perceived by Cragg is one in which the people of the Middle Eastern monotheistic faiths meet in a personal narrative of distinctive intimacy with God. Anti-Semitism is used as the agent of fear that might justify Israeli abuse of Palestinians but "there was, there is, a Semitism that unites us". But Cragg remains aware of the deepest ambiguities in a Semitism that might pose as Zionism or that could on the other hand find opposing expression as Palestinian/Islamic statehood. Faiths, and the nations which claim to embody them, remain persistently in conflict. Of course, there is a *quantitative* distinction between the Nazi assault upon the Jewish people in the Holocaust, or Shoah, and the annihilation of Arab villagers at Dair Yasin in April 1948 by Zionists. But there is no *qualitative* distinction: killing is killing. One million Jews were blown away by the annihilating wind in Auschwitz; two hundred and fifty-two Arab civilians lay dead in Dair Yasin. Palestine was surely not the arena of the Holocaust, but Palestinians have certainly become victims of the Shoah. Anti-Semitism is an assault: Semitism an embrace. Agents of reconciliation like Kenneth Cragg are frequently characterised as romantics. Looking at the Middle East today, we should hope that this view is wrong.

In very many affecting pages of *Semitism*, Cragg characterises Marc Chagall as a truly Jewish and universalist iconographer of hope. Because the imagery of Chagall dominates the Israeli Knesset and the United Nations assembly chamber in New York "we may invoke him to point the way to the humanity that can shed inclusive tears and . . . engage them to the salvation of the world they weep for, alike in the politics that scheme and the values that belong." When referring to the 'piety' of Chagall, Cragg writes affectingly of an artist whose work is "born of loyal, humble, inwardly hallowing identity, moving nevertheless in the whole range of human curiosity and a will to relate as one undeceiving and undeceived." Cragg as scholar, writer and spiritual teacher lives within the same inward hallowing.

A distinctly personal Christmas poem by Bishop Kenneth Cragg is sent to his friends every year, and through this annual message it is always clear to us that he is a poet, even if he is not easy to read. There is insufficient space here to explore the density of his language, but it would be a mistake to ignore his poetry. One poem alone must be sufficient, and it is one that relates to Kenneth's perpetual, life-enhancing dialogue:

A Muslim/Christian Reflection

'Say: had there been angels in the earth going about in tranquillity, We would have sent an angel from heaven as a messenger.'

The Qur'an, Surah 17.95

But we are men. An angel messenger
Might fitly serve as heaven's harbinger
For angel-kind. Our human case demands
The voice of man, the living, working hands
Of traffic in our world, bone of our bone,
Flesh of our flesh, one known as we are known,
Skilled in the truth of us. In peace to walk
Is not our habit. Passions grimly stalk
Through all our centuries. Our flesh is proud,
Our structures harsh, our better reason cowed

By fear or guile, our story marred and stained.
The Word by God's initiative constrained
To seek our low estate must speak our mortal tongue,
In human travail take the human reach of wrong.

SOURCES FOR THE STUDY OF KENNETH CRAGG

Kenneth Cragg, *The Call of the Minaret*, New York 1956.
——, *Sandals at the Mosque*, London 1959.
——, *Alive to God: Muslim and Christian Prayer*, OUP, London 1970.
——, *This Year In Jerusalem*. DLT, London 1982.
——, *Muhammad and the Christian. A Question of Response*. New York 1984.
——, *The Christ and the Faiths*. SPCK, London 1986.
——, *Poetry of the Word at Christmas*, Worthing 1987.
——, *Readings in the Qur'an*, London 1988; Brighton & Portland 1999.
——, *Faith and Life Negotiate. A Christian Story-Study*, Norwich 1994.
——, *Returning to Mount Hira: Islam in Contemporary Terms*, London 1994.
——, *Palestine: The Prize and Price of Zion*. Cassell, London 1997.
——, *Common Prayer: A Muslim–Christian Spiritual Anthology*, Oxford 1999.
——, *Muhammad in the Qur'an: The Task and the Text*, London 2001.
——, *Am I not your Lord? Human Meaning in Divine Question*, London 2002.
——, *A Certain Sympathy of Scriptures*, Brighton & Portland 2004.
——, *Semitism*, Brighton & Portland 2005
Edwyn C. Hoskyns, *Cambridge Sermons*, SPCK, London 1938.
Ed. David Thomas & Clare Amos, *A Faithful Presence, Essays for Kenneth Cragg*, London 2003.

ZIAUDDIN SARDAR

Biographical Outline

"The challenge of being a Muslim today
is the responsibility to harness a controlled
explosion, one that will clear the premises of all the
detritus without damaging the foundations that
would bring down the house of Islam."

Ziauddin Sardar, *British, Muslim, Writer*

ZIAUDDIN SARDAR
WAS BORN IN DIPALPUR,
NORTHERN PAKISTAN IN 1951.

His father emigrated from the Republic of Pakistan to the United Kingdom. After two years of separation the family joined him first in Randlesham Road, then in Hillsea Street, Hackney, London E5, moving on to the seventeenth floor of Seaton Point: a tower block of flats, close to Hackney Downs and Clapton Pond and also in London E5. It was a world where 'Paki-bashing' was common. During his primary years, Zia had a serious bout of rheumatic fever. He was treated for a long time in Hackney Hospital and then spent some months of convalescence in Broadstairs, Kent. As a patient he was also an omnivorous reader. Much later, the Sardar family moved on to Warwick Avenue, which has its own tube station on the Bakerloo Line and is not far from the Edgware Road. Ziauddin Sardar now lives with his wife and children in northwest London.

Ziauddin Sardar first studied at Brooke House Secondary Modern School, Clapton. He became the Science Editor of the national magazine for pupils known as *Sixth Form Opinion*. He moved on to read physics at the City University in London and would emerge as a significant information scientist, correspondent and lecturer.

In the 1970s he was General Secretary of FOSIS, the Federation of Students Islamic Society in UK and Eire, which he described as a "microcosm of the Muslim world in its ethnic and geographical extent as well as its disparate relations to tradition, modernity, revolution and reform". FOSIS included numerous expatriate scholars from many Muslim lands, most of whom were pursuing higher degrees in Great Britain. Supernumeraries in FOSIS included an exotic assortment of 'Islamic' hippies, adhering to some supposed form of Sufism. But the most important later group of Muslims students to emerge in FOSIS were those born of immigrant parents, brought up and educated in the United Kingdom. Sardar belonged to that third bloc. FOSIS were active in their opposition to President Nasser in the 1960s. They opposed the Israeli occupation of the West Bank and Gaza in 1967 and the notorious arson at Jerusalem's al–Aqsa mosque in 1969. Widespread student activism throughout the UK at that time was similar to that exercised by FOSIS.

During the 1970s Sardar studied Islamic theology with Jaffar Sheikh Idris, a distinguished Sudanese theologian and philosopher who had worked on a D.Phil. at Oxford with Karl Popper. Zia admired Idris but came to despair of any mode of Quranic exegesis that ought to have been an 'Open Road' but became 'languished, overgrown and neglected'. Scholars in many faith-systems sympathise with Zia when he deplores 'the blind following of received *unwisdom*'. Sardar moved on to examine Sufism with Sheik Nazim Adil Haqqani but became alienated from that mystical tradition in Islam. Ziauddin felt that Sufism could not produce a viable social order, but tended to degenerate into authoritarianism, with a cult of personality that was wretched. Within an emerging politicised form of Islam, even Abu-Ala Maududi and Sayyid Qutb, the ideologues of the Jammat-e-Islami and the Muslim Brotherhood, disappointed him because they too were narrow and confining. He was searching for a new, developing Muslim civilisation and not for one that had fallen into a pit of primitive dogma. He needed a contemporary Islam rooted firmly in the great tradition but facing the future. Sardar regretted the reality of an Islam 'frozen in history' that 'for centuries . . . has been denied the oxygen of new interpretation'. Worse, Islam's 'thought and tradition – from being dynamic and life enhancing – have been fossilised and preserved in stone.' Some contemporary Christians would find no difficulty in identifying these words as applicable to their own faith-system.

In 1974 Sardar worked in the Hajj Research Centre of King Abdul Aziz University, Jeddah. He undertook his first 'pilgrimage' to Mecca in 1975 and continued to make the Hajj for four more years until 1979. He started to write his first major book in February 1976 and has since occupied a noteworthy position as a contemporary Muslim author, broadcaster, essayist, journalist and reviewer. He has contributed to *Nature*, *New Scientist*, *The Independent*, the *Herald* and *Sunday Herald*, Glasgow, *New Statesman*, *Observer,* the *Muslim World Book Review* and many other publications.

The magazine *Afkar: Inquiry* was conceived and edited by Sardar from June 1984 to September 1987. It became popular with the Muslim intelligentsia, soon selling 50,000 copies per publication. Zia edited the magazine by dividing his monthly commitment into thirds – about ten days at the editorial desk, ten more travelling the Muslim world and a further ten days working at the Centre for Policy and Future Studies at East–West University in Chicago, Illinois. *Afkar: Inquiry* ceased publication in December 1987, but is generally regarded as one of the most significant Muslim/English-language publications in recent times, playing an important part in the development of Zia's own thought.

From early adulthood, through the years with *Afkar: Inquiry,* and right up to the present, Dr. Ziauddin Sardar has been an inveterate traveller. In a personal e-mail to the editors of the *Ziauddin Sardar Reader* on 23 October 2001, Sardar tells of a 1980 invitation to Ottawa by a group of Canadian Muslim scientists and professionals. He was already known as the author of *The Future of Muslim Civilisation* (1979) and many Muslims wished to hear him. Sardar noted that he was surprised that there was no one at Ottawa airport to meet him. He waited for half an hour and then rang the contact number, and was told that the whole group was at the airport waiting to be introduced to him. He noted the description of the party, quickly spotted them and went over to introduce himself. But a member of the group said that they must excuse him: they were looking for someone important. They brushed him aside. For a second time Ziauddin Sardar introduced himself but the reception party were irritated. He did not seem to understand that they were waiting for 'an important writer from London':

> STANDING IN FRONT OF THEM HE SAID – 'I am here. You are waiting for me.'
> A BRIEF INTERROGATION FOLLOWED:
> 'Are you Ziauddin Sardar?'
> 'Yes'.
> 'Are you the author of *The Future of Muslim Civilisation?*'
> 'Yes, I am. But you are clearly disappointed.'
> 'No. No. We expected someone much older. Someone with a beard. Perhaps someone with an arching back.'

Maybe the age, the beard and the bent back are merely metaphors for a 'classical' Muslim scholar, though the icon of Ziauddin – energetic, unbent, pony-tailed and beardless – is admired and reviled in equal measure. Certainly, he has travelled everywhere: visiting Muslim communities in Africa, China, Iran, Malaysia, Pakistan, Saudi Arabia and Turkey. He knows many other secular societies extremely well, even though they are not within the 'House of Islam'. In Iran, Zia was physically and mentally abused; in Pakistan he had some lively exchanges with President Zia-ul-Haq whom he had earlier described as 'a deranged dictator' but who gave him a farewell gift of a table lamp made of solid green marble, packed in a wooden case –'Think of it as the burden of the Shariah!'; and in Malaysia he was close to the liberal deputy prime minister of the country, Anwar Ibrahim, who was imprisoned by Mahathir Muhammad, the obsessive and rather extreme premier of the country, so that Zia had to flee from the Malaya peninsula.

Perhaps the gentlest story in *Desperately Seeking Paradise* (2004) concerns a Sufi sheikh in Konya, Turkey. Sardar asks the sheikh, 'What is Islam?' The answer from the Sufi master is one that might seem either weighty or exasperating, or both: 'Islam is wearing a beard, a trench coat and a turban.'

Professor Ziauddin Sardar is presently the Editor of both *Futures* and *Third Text*. He is a special Correspondent for the *New Statesman* and Professor of Postcolonial Studies, Department of Arts Policy and Management, The City University London. His personal journey as a questioning Muslim has been characterised as a subtle individual attempt to initiate a moderate, humane course between modern secularism and the affirmed certainties of the Islamic faith in which he was raised: 'I don't take being a Muslim as a given for me, being a Muslim is a challenge.'

Listening to Islam

with

Ziauddin Sardar

"Muslim people have been on the verge of
physical, cultural and intellectual
extinction simply because they
have allowed parochialism and
and petty traditionalism to
rule their minds. We must
break free from the
ghetto mentality."

Ziauddin Sardar, *Reformist Ideas and Muslim Intellectuals*

PROFESSOR ZIAUDDIN SARDAR
IS A POLYMATH. THERE ARE
MANY THINGS TO LEARN FROM HIM

and other things that Muslim traditionalists might think that we ought not to learn from him. He has been bitterly attacked by some Muslim scholars, especially those conservatives or purists who have their own websites. He is a master of scientific sophistication, with a finely tuned critical mind. Dr. Sardar has written extensively about the modern world, with a spiky and aggressive timbre. Many of his readers find him politically persuasive. He convinces some, but is derided by others. A handful of modern Muslim theologians have commented that he sometimes seems to prefer evasion or carefully calculated ambiguity to standard textual commentary. But a characteristic comment from this modern Muslim intellectual – in *Today's Problems, Tomorrow's Solutions* (1988) – has real force: "There cannot be a living dynamic, thriving Muslim civilisation without a body of critical and creative intellectuals."

During *Islam Awareness Week* (22–28 November 2004) Sardar gave a lecture on *Ilm, Islam and the Internet*. It is *ilm*, the pursuit of knowledge, which was once the driving force of classical Muslim civilisation, and Sardar hopes that the quest may be revived in the future: "the Qur'an employs the word *ilm* more than eight hundred times and devotes a third of the text to praising reason, reflection, research, scholarship, travel and virtually every form of communication known at the time." Zia examines *ilm* as holistic knowledge in the sense of being connected with everything. *Ilm* is a form of *ibadah* (worship): "an hour of contemplation is better than a year of worship." In his estimate one-third of the Qur'an is devoted to some form of knowledge, and the reduction of *ilm* to religious knowledge alone would be a failure. Interrogation of the holy book should also involve interrogation of Muslim sources, even on the Internet. A dynamic interpretation of Islam is needed. One Quranic example of a straightforward devotional petition must suffice:

Surah Ta Ha 20 *aya* 114 (Perhaps the title *Ta Ha* is not to be understood as isolated letters, but as the vocative 'O man' in one

Arabic dialect): "Oh my Lord, advance me in knowledge." (Ali) "Lord, increase me in knowledge" (Haleem). "Lord, increase me in knowledge" (Cragg). "O my Sustainer, cause me to grow in knowledge!" (Asad).

Sardar is an information scientist. His personal description of his profession – once given to Iranian State Security – is an understatement, but it is excellent and amusing: "an information scientist is someone who handles, processes, stores and retrieves information. He is a sort of glorified librarian who knows how to use computers."

Muslims are related to the text of the Qur'an no matter what the interpretation. In Zia Sardar's own words, "the Qur'an speaks to me in its totality." *Al-Alaq*, the first *Surah* of the Qur'an delivered to the prophet on twenty-seventh of Ramadan in the year 611 CE, focuses upon knowledge imparted by God. Reading and writing – the transcript and the knowledge received – help to define Muslim culture and society. From a modern Muslim point-of-view, without the communication and the transmission there could be no true Islamic society. We understand the notion conveyed by the *Introduction* to *Islam, Postmodernism and Other Futures* (2003), which firmly states: "Sardar desires Islam to move forward as a civilisation based on participatory governance and social justice, and as a knowledge-based society committed to the worship of God and the creation of technical, scientific, and philosophical knowledge that can improve the human condition not just of . . . the community of believers, but of humanity as a whole. While his vision is distinctively Islamic, it is also intrinsically humanistic." Professor Ziauddin Sardar's vision of Islam is far from mystical Islam or fundamentalist interpretations: contemporary Muslim scholars struggle to see beyond both. His appeal is for the classical polymath to be rediscovered by contemporary Muslim intellectuals, who must become their modern counterparts. They must be the ones who will reshape Muslim civilisation, as it was once shaped in the classical period.

Sardar relates, in an altogether personal manner, to the central intellectual debates of Islam carried out from the end of the ninth century to the beginning of the sixteenth. In this context it is only possible to list a handful of Islam's greatest intellectuals in this period: Al-Kindi (d. circa 866–873) was the author of over two hundred books on mathematics, physics, medicine and philosophy. He served as tutor to the Caliph's son in the Abbasid court in Baghdad and was known as the 'first philosopher of the Arab people'. Al-Kindi was carefully schooled in Greek philosophy. Ibn Sina (980–1037: *Avicenna*) was an encyclopaedist from Central Asia, a physician and psychologist, who taught that Reason could lead to ultimate truth. He was a major influence upon European philosophy and especially on St. Thomas Aquinas (1224–74). Ibn Rushd (1126–98: *Averroes*) was a physician and scientist who set out to integrate Aristotelian philosophy with Islamic thought. Al-Ghazzali (1058–1111: *Algazel*) was one of the greatest Islamic jurists, theologians and mystical thinkers in Islam. He abandoned his career to embrace the ecstatic state of *fana*, devoting his life to Sufism which believes that the ideal human being is the mirror of God's attributes – union with God is sought by *fana*, the annihilation of the self and the ego into God. Ibn Khaldun (1332–1406) was the greatest Arab historian of any period and is regarded as the originator of modern sociology. His magnum opus was entitled *Kitab al-Ibar* ('The book exemplifying universal history'). The *Muqaddimah* is his lengthy introduction to the comprehensive history of the world. It was written in 1377 and became known in Europe as the *Prolegomena*. Ibn Khaldun outlines a cyclic view of history, explaining the reasons for the rise and fall of civilisations in terms of nomadic and sedentary modes of existence. Creating a stable God-fearing community can break the cycle. These five exemplary Muslim scholars are intimations of the extraordinary depth of Islam's intellectual history.

Sardar cannot see Islam "as a set of rituals, a list of do's and don'ts, a code of rigid, unchanging regulations and laws". For him Islam is "not just a religion; it is a worldview based on a matrix of values and concepts." He is following this great tradition by attempting the type of leap forward in Islamic thought that can only benefit modern thought in general and the Islamic world in particular, though it would be important to notice that Islam as a world religion is as fragmented as Christianity. It is true that some modern Islamic philosophy wishes to establish a distinctive form of philosophy that would provide some kind of agenda for unity in the *umma* (the whole people of Islam). But there is an equally powerful tradition today that seeks to identify Islamic philosophy with illuminationist and mystical thought in the Sufi tradition. Perhaps the most powerful contemporary influence is Seyyed Hussein Nasr: he has a profound knowledge of western scientific thought and develops a spiritual–mystical approach to the natural world:

"Only the revival of a spiritual conception of nature that is based on intellectual and metaphysical doctrines can help to neutralise the havoc brought about by the applications of modern science and integrate this science itself into a more universal perspective."

Professor Seyyed Hussein Nasr has held major academic posts in Iran and the United States, and has introduced some Western concepts into Shia Islam. But it is also certain that there are many Muslim thinkers in the twenty-first century who wish to employ all the techniques and approaches of contemporary thought but without the mystical baggage.

In his contribution to *Futures* (28/1996), Professor Sardar focuses once again upon knowledge and upon science in particular. One of his icons, who is the principal hero in this piece, is the seminal Islamic scientist and philosopher Abu Rayhan al-Biruni (973–1048) who became known as *al-ustad*, 'the teacher'. He was a Persian from Transoxiana who studied Hindu technology, astronomy and mathematics in India, though his acquisition of Indian thought also led him on to explore pharmacology, botany, history and optics: using his own instruments, al-Biruni calculated the radius of the Earth, which he knew to be round, to within ten miles of its actual measurement. What Sardar is telling us is that he too shares al-Biruni's notion that there are no disciplinary boundaries: disciplines are 'artificial constructs' and all of life is 'a process of learning'. There is no particular methodology that is specifically Muslim, nor is it anti-Muslim. Different methods may prove a single point. For this particular Muslim scholar it is most important to engage with the world, understand it, change it and even reform it: he is not living in the past or assuming that all modernity is equally transparent. The only future for some Muslims/Christians is Paradise/Heaven – or the imagined alternative – but for all Sardar's contemporary Muslims "time within Islamic cosmology is 'future time' with 'futures consciousness'."

Christians who listen to Ziauddin Sardar must begin with his brand of Islamic theology: opening-up his theology could simply mean opening the Qur'an. The Qur'an is the very Word of God, transmitted by the Angel Gabriel in Arabic through Muhammad. Monotheism is at the centre of the text but other social, political and legal essentials are present in the holy book. Zia was taught to read the text in Arabic, a task he completed at the age of fourteen, though his mother tongue was Urdu. The Qur'an is untranslatable. No other language carries the full range of meaning, which the Arabic Qur'an alone can convey. Any translation is an interpretation. That is all. Sardar read the Qur'an in the English translation of M. Marmaduke Pickthall, a convert to Islam. (Muslim converts to Christianity and Christian converts to Islam have never understood that conversion is always formed in denial and rarely if ever resolves into affirmation). Modern Muslim statisticians state that less than 15 per cent of Muslims know Arabic, and that this percentage is shrinking. If Arabic is not understood, can anything theological, spiritual or mystical be understood? The numinous miracle of *Qur'anan arabiyyan* – the Arabic recitation – is certainly one of the greatest wonders amongst all the world religions. *Qur'an* can indeed mean 'that which is to be recited'. No other historical religious text enjoys such importance because of the language in which it was written and through which it exists, and Sardar is right when he says that the accent is always on memorising the text of the Qur'an rather than understanding it. Two central theological concepts in Islam are absent from Sardar's *Introducing Islam* (2001). *Tanzil* is the sending down of the contents of the Qur'an into the mind and upon the lips of the prophet Muhammad. *Umm al-Kitab* ('the mother of the book') is the eternal counterpart of the Qur'an. It was perfectly delivered to Muhammad in the last twenty years of his life. Sardar uses the phrase rather loosely in connection with *Surah 1 Al-Fatiha*, the first chapter of the Qur'an, which is translated as 'The Opening' in most English versions. Muslim Orthodoxy perceives the *Umm al-Kitab* as the entire *Qur'an* revealed directly in a human language. Reciting and reading the sacred text is to live within it.

Although it might be inappropriate to compare Dr. Sardar with the radical Christian theologian Rudolf Bultmann (1884–1976), who sought to 'demythologise' the gospel texts, it is true that Zia often speaks of an 'interpretative relationship with the Qur'an' in which each generation must 'reinterpret the textual sources in the light of its own experience.' Bultmann's aim to make a religious message intelligible in the modern world has been widely respected. It is a lamentable fact that many great Muslim scholars – Egyptian, Syrian and Iranian – who have devoted their lives to the study and exegesis of their holy book, have felt obliged to interpret the Qur'an by using pseudonyms. They fear death for heresy, even in the twenty-first century. Sardar believes that a certain liberation comes to Muslims by redefining the basic conditions of interpretation in the House of Islam, which should also involve 'recognition of the Qur'an as a Word of God': the use of the indefinite article must be devastating for traditionalists. But reinterpretation is essential for contemporary Muslims: 'If this generation fails to do so it undermines one of its basic God-given freedoms: the freedom to re-understand the divine text in its own epoch.' Perhaps Ziauddin Sardar is right, but we cannot be sure. Could the elementary question applied by Professor Hodgson to the Christian Scriptures be applied to the Qur'an? *'What must the truth be, and have been, if it appeared like that to men who thought and wrote as they did?'*, and might this question be applied to the Qur'an? The answer, in relation to the concept of *Tanzil* and in the face of the *Umm al-Kitab*, must surely be 'No'. In a further development of interpretation, Professor Sardar is firm in his conviction that Islamic jurisprudence (*Fiqh*) – covering all aspects of religious, political and civil life – requires careful contemporary exegesis: "Once liberated from the confines of a suffocating and outdated *fiqh*, Islam can develop a more humane face and, hence, remove the humanitarian distrust that so many Christians have of Islam." He is not entirely alone in perceiving Tradition as a dynamic, not a static or fossilised outlook, but Muslim 'puritans' and literary romantics must distrust him: they certainly make him feel uncomfortable.

In his important paper, *The Ethical Connection: Christian–Muslim Relations in the Postmodern Age* – delivered at the Centre for the Study of Islam and Christian–Muslim Relations at Selly Oak in Birmingham, 1990 – Dr. Sardar dismisses modern and postmodern philosophy, mysticism, and social-activism but affirms the traditionalism of the Cambridge theologian Brian Hebblethwaite: "God must be thought of as infinite and absolute, if he is indeed to be both metaphysically adequate ground and explanation of the world's being and also a religiously adequate object of worship." Sardar is in the same camp as Hebblethwaite but believes above all that Christian–Muslim cooperation involves the interpretation of a working monotheistic ethics: Sardar is sadly rather dismissive of those like Bishop Kenneth Cragg, in his *Alive to God*, who seek first of all for a 'real togetherness' in 'common prayer'. He prefers to focus upon Believers who 'need to be where the action is'. The notion of prayer as inaction could not appeal to any who believe that there is only one God, and that Muslims and Christians can believe in and pray to the same God, but Sardar's priority in the field of Christian Muslim co-operation is to "seek a joint under-standing of the will of this God and to shape the human world and human history in accordance with this will".

A further turning point in Sardar's thought – his preoccupation with postmodernism and the West – arose from the appearance of Salman Rushdie's 1988 novel *The Satanic Verses*. It is a book that Dr. Sadar hated, but it is a book that creates hysteria amongst many Muslims, even the liberal Muslims – and 'liberal' is a word Ziauddin prefers to use of himself. When reading the novel he felt that 'the inner sanctum' of his 'identity' had been despoiled. Why any prominent Muslim intellectual should be concerned about such a novel is something of a mystery. Sardar understandably objects to Rushdie's abuse of the life and the name of Muhammad. It must of course be acknowledged that the real example of the Prophet is a source of Muslim identity for many Muslims. *The Satanic Verses* is a post-modern and therefore secular work. It is hardly a major work of fiction.

D. H. Lawrence (1885–1930) wrote a short novel about Jesus after the Crucifixion, with the contrived and obscene punning title *The Escaped Cock* (1929). After much debate Lawrence's novel was renamed *The Man Who Died*. It tells of a 'resurrected', 'revived' Christ in love with a priestess of Isis. Passages of physical sexuality have prominence. Like Rushdie's *The Satanic Verses*, Lawrence's *The Man Who Died* is indecent. The consequence of this kind of fiction is far from clear. For the believers it probably has no significance. It is not read. Blasphemy in Lawrence and Rushdie is a complete irrelevance. What is not irrelevant is the advice given to British Muslim readers that they should kill Salman Rushdie. Although Evangelical Christians might easily have wished to kill D. H. Lawrence they would probably not even have read his novella, but Islam, in an official form, decided to kill the author of *The Satanic Verses*. On 14 February 1989 the Ayatollah Khomeini applied a sentence of death upon Rushdie in his legal *fatwa* (a judgement or formal ruling based upon Islamic law in Iran). This is an alarming misrepresentation of authentic Islam, though Dr. Sardar himself is quite certain that forgiving Rushdie is impossible. The underlying hysteria in response to Rushdie's novel could never be clear to most Westerners, whether bursting with religious conviction or clouded in complete scepticism. But the Iranian Head of State had successfully provoked confrontation between Muslims and secularists – to an extent between East and West – and especially between believers and unbelievers. Those who regarded their faith-system as an absolute conviction and those who saw all religion as mere credulity were set against each other. As Kenneth Cragg observed in *Troubled by Truth* (1992), "We have seen the worst of both worlds – an irate Islam in hue and cry against a writer (and) a liberal establishment in urgent self-exoneration of any liability for it." It certainly needed to be understood that secularism occupied the centre in all European societies. Ziauddin Sardar was especially angry with the radical secular novelist Fay Weldon. She clearly knew little about any religion. But she was confident that the Qur'an was a limited and limiting text, abusive of unbelief with an instruction to kill unbelievers. Zia did not see Weldon's outburst as an isolated incident. Within the British secular society of the late 1980s he felt that he was being brutalised from both sides. The combined forces of the liberal inquisition and Muslim fanaticism were overrunning him. He was more than usually outraged when a Muslim leader in Britain began encouraging young Muslim to answer the call of Khomeini's *fatwa*: "I was being brutalised from both sides. I was being overrun by the combined forces of the liberal inquisition and Muslim fanaticism. I felt my humanity seeping out of me." Sardar relates the confrontation between

Salman Rushdie and the Ayatollah Khomeini to an old Malay proverb in which two elephants fight on the grass, and the grass between the two is trampled. The conclusion is extraordinarily poignant and affecting, but more than a little perplexing for some of his co-religionists: 'I am the grass. It is me they are fighting over . . . for somewhere between these two extremes was the humanistic interpretation of Islam . . . that I had worked endlessly to construct.'

On the recent feast of 'Id al–Adha (21 January 2005) the present leader of the Islamic Republic of Iran – a leading Shi'ite cleric who had taken the mantle of Ayatollah Khomeini – continued to urge Muslim pilgrims in Mecca to kill Salman Rushdie.

In the political contributions from Professor Sardar the principal emphasis lies in an analysis of America's perception of itself. A secondary but equally important investigation concerns the way in which modern Islam sees itself and also how it is seen by the rest of the world. It is of considerable importance for those in the West to attempt to understand how a sensitive, modern Muslim really feels about the United States and about the lethal coalition attack upon Iraqi civilians. *Why Do People Hate America?* was written by Ziauddin Sardar and Merryl Wyn Davies (2002) and outlines the possible reasons for this hatred, offering an appropriate examination of Muslim hurt following the events on 11 September 2001.

Why Do People Hate America? is at times certainly didactic and pedantic but it is a fast read and is packed with useful information, which benefits all. The four main reasons for hating America involve the use of loan words from philosophy and theology, and some of them probably need unscrambling: *existential, cosmological, ontological* and finally *'definitions'*. America is a 'hyperpower', so dominant that it shapes the lives of all the people on Earth. The *existential* condition of Third World nations – physical, political and cultural – is a cause for hostility towards America, which is perceived as literally taking food out of the mouths of the people of the developing world. The *cosmological* alludes to America as the prime cause of everything: 'the tallest tree attracts the most dangerous winds during a typhoon'. Mathieu Kassovitz's film *La Haine* (*Hate*, 1995) shows three teenagers looking at an advert with the caption 'The World is Yours.' They delete the 'Y', conveying their message that 'the world' does not in fact include them: it belongs to the nation that has reconstructed the world through its own military and economic power. This is the cosmological argument. The *ontological* argument in this book explains the nature of American *being* as the only good and virtuous nation, fighting against the inherent evil of terrorism. The politico-religious America of Bush appropriates goodness to itself, assuming that God identifies with the born-again clique in the White House. American certainty of its own goodness and of the evil terrorist antithesis is so confident that 'hatred breeds hatred'. The fourth reason for hating America is that it *defines* itself as a just and free democracy, though in the authors' view America is best understood solely in terms of self-interest. Values ought to be *defined* in a variety of ways, but the values of the current war are imposed values. One aphorism is well known – 'it is better to have a just unIslamic state than an unjust Islamic one'. But the search for justice eludes us.

It was interesting to note that this book contains a mass of references to the NBC television programme *The West Wing*, which stars Martin Sheen as President Bartlet. Many find hope in the ideal of Barlet's American liberal values and democratic culture, compared with the delusions of Bush/Blair. In one notable episode, and bearing in mind the necessity of a simple story line on television or stage, a test blank appears in the sentence written on a white board: 'Islamic extremist is to Islam what _ _ _ is to Christianity'. The answer given is 'KKK': *That's what we're talking about – the Klu Klux Klan gone medieval and global. It could not have less to do with Islamic men and women of faith, of whom there are millions and millions.*' The assertion of 'difference' even in a brief snatch on TV makes sense, and an American e-mail from Montana in the United States to Khaaled al-Maeena, editor-in-chief of Saudi Arabia's *Arab News,* is unsettling but unsurprising: 'I hate you all. The Qur'an is the book of Satan, the devil, the teachings of evil, the book that is used to justify murder. Anyone who worships Islam is the devil's child. There will be a great conflict in the future, a conflagration between Islam and Christianity, and the crusaders of Christianity will rid the world of the Satanic hell that is Islam . . .' It can be no surprise that the British Islamic extremist group known as *Hizb ut-Tahrir* produced a leaflet in 2001 which stated that: 'All Muslims are duty bound to fight the unbelievers . . . the only solution is *jihad*, which is to be understood purely as '*qitaal*' (fighting).' Religiously motivated hatred is so common that no further comment is required. Racism too cannot be a minor issue. Recalling the childhood 'Paki-bashing' of Ziauddin Sadar, it may be asked, 'Within the monotheistic faiths, which – Christianity, Islam or Judaism – are entirely free from Racism?' The answer can only be 'none'.

The book concludes – and it might be noted that one author is a Muslim by birth and the other a convert to Islam – with an aggressive edge and pacific appeal. America is 'the source of global hatred' but a viable and sane future can only be found by 'transcending hatred'. America is called to 'carry the responsibility' of moving us all beyond hatred. For Sardar and Davies this involves unwrapping the United States from its flag and enveloping itself in the last four lines of *Why Do People Hate America?* (A rough-and-ready pop-music adaptation of words originating from the 'peace prayer' of St. Francis of Assisi).

> O Master, grant that I may never seek
> So much to be consoled as to console,
> To be understood as to understand,
> To be loved, as to love, with all my soul.

American Dream, Global Nightmare (2004) is another political work by Professor Ziauddin Sardar and Merryl Wyn Davies. This book attempts to show that there is something seriously wrong with twenty-first century America, in which the *dream* has become a *nightmare* from which the world needs to awake. *The Ten Laws of American Mythology* defined in the text require close analysis, but they are only persuasive 'laws' in their American context.

Law 1: *Fear is essential.* 'Without fear there is no America' and "recourse to fear is the motivating force that determines its actions and reactions."

Law 2: *Escape is the reason for being.* America is "founded on the premise of escape from one's self." It is a place where the individual citizen may remake one's self in an idealised form.

Law 3: *Ignorance is bliss.* The vision of American 'exceptionality' – of its uniqueness, outstanding decency and atypical character – is the ecstasy induced by lack of wisdom.

Law 4: *America is the idea of nation.* Patriotism and nationalism are the foundation of American life.

Law 5: *Democratisation of everything is the essence of America.* The process ranges from 'fast food to fast fashion, violence and gun laws to access to pornography.' This idea of democratisation in process means 'America'.

Law 6: *American democracy has the right to be imperial and express itself through empire.* Far from being truly democratic, the American practices of imperialism and empire have existed since the origins of the state. Sardar and Davies may be less guilty than Bush and Blair in their simplistic view of the world in black and white, but we know that American power is wreaking havoc on Earth, and that American 'exceptionality' is a delusion. The number of people voting for Bush in 2004 is much smaller than the majority of those citizens who do not, would not or cannot vote. The numbers of those voting for Kerry were close to those for Bush. Most citizens have no role in the American processes of citizenship or 'exceptionality'.

Law 7: *Cinema is the engine of empire.* In the light of Arnold Schwarzenegger's election as Governor of an American State – and the current attempts to allow a foreigner of extreme right-wing origin and misogynistic tendency to become an American President – perhaps it is not mistaken to imagine the authentic icon of the United States today as Schwarzenneger in *Terminator* 'slaying and demolishing whatever may come or stand in its way.'

Law 8: *Celebrity is the common currency of empire.* American celebrities of one kind or another – from Oscar winners, who appear on the world's TV screens, to American military leaders who operate across the Earth – are demonstrations of global power.

Law 9: *War is necessity.* Economic, technological, scientific, cultural and religious domination are an obligation for America and its 'reason to be.'

Law 10: *American tradition and history are universal narratives applicable across all time and space*. Global hegemony is synonymous with American domination.

Perhaps the generalising – even trivialising – presentation of these 'laws' appears to be too simplistic, but Sardar and Davies have understood our present predicament. It is quite certain that the solitary empire controlled by George W. Bush is indeed an imposition upon the United Kingdom, the Third World and the Middle East. But these 'laws' are most obviously potent when the reader of *American Dream, Global Nightmare* reflects upon the military might thrown against Iraqi cities such as Fallujah. In these places too many non-combatants die and most of them are women and children.

American Dream, Global Nightmare is structured around Hollywood movies as metaphors of reassuring and terrifying visions. John Ford's *Drums Along the Mohawk* (1939) anticipates the conquest of the real and imagined wilderness. *To Have and Have Not* by Howard Hawks (1944) anticipates 'law four' where patriotism and nationalism are the foundation of life. Allan Dwan's *Sands of Iwo Jima* (1949) celebrates military prowess, the love of war and the use of force. Robert Altman's *The Player* (1992), Roland Emmerich's *Universal Soldier* (1992) and even *Groundhog Day* (1993) include interpretations that are confined to show business, the failure to characterise American culture and a global narrative where even the republicans and democrats do not know the difference between an aggressive war and fantasy. The outlines of these movies may be far too simplistic but they are amusing, especially when the writers come to realise that Robert Altman's *The Player* is a multi-layered, complicated and individualistic movie and therefore not entirely unlike the many other Hollywood products outlined in the text.

At a deeper level, this book discusses the neo-conservative narratives of Francis Fukuyama (*The End of History and the Last Man*, 1992) and Philip Bobbitt (*The Shield of Achilles*, 2002), which appear to have been formulated to undermine the variety of nations, cultures and religious faiths. The notion that 'Islamic

Fundamentalism' is the only kind of Islam is nonsense, but Fukuyama equates the new extremism of Sayyid Qutb and terrorism with all that is Muslim. Islam is in reality a richly seamed faith and it is the link between culture and religion that makes 'the culture a stubborn form of resistance to the spread of American imperialism'. It is almost impossible to distinguish between the *Islamic* or *Bushite* evangelical religious fundamentalisms, though President Jacques Chirac of France and Secretary General Kofi Annan of the United Nations both appear to have a clear grasp of the two competing theologies of annihilation, and perhaps of the endless destruction and death that await us. Who can answer the central question posed by Davies and Sardar, 'When the empire has had its fill, what will remain for the rest of humanity?'

Why Do People Hate America? with *American Dream, Global Nightmare* are both international bestsellers. They have made a significant contribution to our thinking about the world as we see it now. Iraq haunts us; as do the dark dreams of death in Indonesia, suffering in Darfur, fear in Chechnya and alienation in Iraq. These are the global nightmares shared by all mankind. Ziauddin Sardar continues to play an important role as a journalist with the *New Statesman, The Independent* and other publications. The singular advantage of his journalism is that he clearly understands the role of Muslim extremists, who have lost all vestiges of humanity, and the equally disturbing role of American British intrusion in the Muslim world. With liberal Muslims everywhere, he has always identified Muslim terrorists as those who are amongst the must dehumanised people on the planet. But there is a question of balance between Muslim and Christian fundamentalists. We may live in an interconnected world, but the empire – the American Bushite Empire – always strikes back with its 'lethal righteousness'. The British in particular do not surrender to the make-believe imperial power of Islam, but the present New Labour government has handed too much authority to United States imperialism. The inhuman future that awaits most people might be Islamic terrorism, but it might equally involve the use of imperialistic military power as the sole means of addressing the complex issues that face mankind. Much 'religion' equals international terrorism. Mark Juergensmeyer's

Terror in the Mind of God. The Global Rise of Religious Violence (2000) documents the worldwide growth of religious terrorism and manages to understand the strange magnetism between religious conviction and aggression.

As a moderate Muslim, Sardar is wise to avoid the condemnation of Christian Fundamentalism. But Christians themselves best know the reality of Christian terrorism. The fanaticism of Orange Protestantism is not different from Roman Catholic nationalism. The destructive forces of Serbian Orthodoxy and Islamic extremism throughout the Balkans are both firmly rooted in violence. Half of the world's most dangerous terrorist groups claim religion alone as their motivation. No one who really cares about matters of faith can afford to ignore the dangers that lurk within the norms of doctrinal extremism. Abortion Clinic bombings and murders, the 'Christian' terrorism of Timothy McVeigh in Oklahoma, and a multitude of varying forms of Christian assault, are in no sense dissimilar to Islamic terrorism. Fundamentalism of most kinds identifies itself as 'religious': a recent CBS poll found that 67 per cent of those who voted for Bush in 2004 did not believe in the theory of evolution but preferred to support Biblical Fundamentalism. In the interests of supporting extremist political activism against standard scientific theory, Bush himself denied the theories of Charles Darwin in the service of religious politics. He was in the company of Sayyid Qutb.

Ziauddin Sardar is one who argues continuously for the creation of political space in which peaceful engagement and hope is the real antidote for doctrinal extremism and active terrorism. He wishes, above all, to refresh and reform Islam as a progressive, pluralistic faith. Most modern Muslims have seen the events of 11 September 2001 as a wake-up call. Since then numerous groups have emerged with the specific goal of containing radical Islam and building civic societies in countries that are predominantly Muslim. Indonesia and Malaysia are good examples. The Republic of Indonesia established a *Liberal Islamic Network* to counter-balance radical Muslim organisations and Malaysia initiated a wide-ranging program called *Progressive Islam*, which redefines Islam's role in education, economics, politics and society. The modern Christian thinker should be encouraged to undertake a similar examination of American Fundamentalism and its destructive force in the West. The political journalism of Sardar is not wasted.

Dr. Sardar once described himself as a 'sceptical' Muslim and it is true that he is critical, and unafraid to question 'religious truths' that seem unconvincing. Many believers, imprisoned in some ways within their own faith-system, understand precisely what Zia means when he says, 'Internalised Islam is the essence of my true Muslim identity.' We might identify Professor Ziauddin Sardar with a legendary Sufi Master, Maruf Karkhi.

When the famous Islamic mystic was approached by one of his Sufi disciples Karkhi was told; "I have been talking to people about you. The Jews say you are one of their own. The Christians consider you to be one of their saints. The Muslims look up to you as a glory to Islam." Maruf Karkhi replied, "That is what they say here in Baghdad. In Jerusalem the Jews called me a Christian. The Christians in Damascus said I was a Muslim. The Muslims in Cairo dubbed me a Jew."

"Then what are we to think of you?" the disciple asked.

"Think of me as a man who said this about himself: 'Those who do not understand me revere me. Those who revile me do not understand me either.'"

Kenneth Cragg, Thomas Merton, Sayyid Qutb and Ziauddin Sardar are hardly amongst those who think that they are what their friends or enemies say that they are, because they know themselves.
Listening to Islam with them is not only important,
it is a privilege.

SOURCES FOR THE STUDY OF ZIAUDDIN SARDAR

Philip Bobbitt, *The Shield of Achilles: War, Peace and the Course of History*, Allen Lane, London 2002.

Ed. Sohail Inayatullah and Gail Boxwell, *Islam, Postmodernism and Other Futures, A Ziauddin Sardar Reader*, Pluto Press, London 2003.

Francis Fukuyama, *The End of History and the Last Man*, Hamish Hamilton, London 1992.

Futures, the journal of policy, planning and future studies, ed. Ziauddin Sardar. E-mail: futures@ziasardar.com

Ed. A. O. Naseef, *Today's Problems, Tomorrow's Solutions*, Mansell, London 1988.

Seyyed Hossein Nasr, *Man and Nature. The Spiritual Crisis in Modern Man*, Unwin, London 1968.

Ziauddin Sardar, *The Future of Muslim Civilisation*, Croom Helm, London 1979.

——, *Islamic Futures: The Shape of Ideas to Come*, London 1985.

——, *Natural Born Futurist*, Futures 28, 1996.

——, *Introducing Islam*, Totem Books, 2001 (Illustrations: Zafar Abbas Malik).

—— and Merryl Wyn Davies, *Why Do People Hate America?* London 2002.

——, *Desperately Seeking Paradise. Journeys of a Sceptical Muslim*, Granta, London 2004.

—— and Merryl Wyn Davies, *American Dream, Global Nightmare*, London 2004.

—— and Merryl Wyn Davies, *The No-nonsense Guide to Islam*, London 2004.

Ed. Juliet Steyn, *Other Than Identity: The Subject, Politics and Art*, Manchester University Press, 1996.

Third Text, journal of visual art and culture. Ed. Ziauddin Sardar. E-mail: third-text@btponeworld.com

SOURCES

*The Qur'an in Translation and
Quranic References*

Books and articles quoted or cited in the text are used under the usual fair use allowances. They are acknowledged with full publication credits in the lists below.

Quotations from the oeuvre of Thomas Merton ocso are used with the permission of the Merton Legacy Trust and the Thomas Merton Centre at Bellarmine University. Sayyid Qutb is adapted into modern English from on-line sources, including, *Milestones* (Signposts on the way): <http://gemsofislamism.tripod.com/ milestones.html> and <http://www.youngmus-lims.ca/online-library/books/milestones>. The same texts appear to have been modified and edited in the paperback edition of *Milestones* (American Trust Publications, revised December 1991 – translator anonymous – ISBN 0892590769). Quotations from Kenneth Cragg are used with the author's permission. Excerpts from the work of Ziauddin Sardar are also quoted with the author's permission.

MERTON SOURCES

PAGE

p. 2 Thomas Merton, *The Monastic Journey*. Sheed Andrews and McMeel, Kansas 1977, p. 157.

p. 4 Thomas Merton, *The Seven Storey Mountain*. Harcourt Brace Jovanovich, New York, 1948, p. 422.

p. 4 Patrick Hart & Jonathan Montaldo, *A Path through Thomas Merton's Journals* in *The Intimate Merton. His Life from His Journals*. Lion Publishing, Oxford 2000, p. 10.

p. 4 Ibid., p. 166.

p. 5 Thomas Merton, *Faith and Violence: Christian Teaching and Christian Practice*. University of Notre Dame Press, Indiana, 1969, p. 215.

p. 5 *The Asian Journal of Thomas Merton*. New Directions, New York, 1973 (Entry 4 December 1968, Colombo), pp. 233–6.

p. 6 Flavian Burns, *Thomas Merton, Monk. A Monastic Tribute*. Image Books, Doubleday, New York 1976, p. 219.

p. 8 Thomas Merton, *Conjectures of a Guilty Bystander*. Sheldon Press, London 1977, pp. 190–1.

p. 9 Thomas Merton: Letters on Religious Experience and Social Concerns. Ed. Wm. Shannon, *The Hidden Ground of Love*. Farrar, Strauss & Giroux, New York, 1985, p. 53.

p. 10 Martin Lings, *What is Sufism?* George Allen & Unwin, London 1975, p. 7.

p. 10 John Baldock, *The Essence of Sufism*. Eagle Editions, London 2004, p. 11.

p. 10 The phrase 'Die before you die' is generally attributed to St. John of the Cross (1542–91).

p. 11 Kenneth Cragg, *The Wisdom of the Sufis*. Sheldon Press, London 1976, p. 28.

p. 11 Ibid., p. 3.

p. 11 Ed. R. Baker & G. Henry, *Merton and Sufism. The Untold Story. A Complete Compendium,*. Fons Vitae, Kentucky, 1999. Editor's note, p. 1.

p. 12 Ibid. Seyyed Hossein Nasr, p. 10.

p. 12 Ibid. Seyyed Hossein Nasr, p. 12.

p. 13 *The Hidden Ground of Love*, p. 454.

p. 13 *Merton and Sufism. The Untold Story. A Complete Compendium*, Gray Henry, p. 166.

p. 13 Ibid., pp. 163–81.

p. 14 *The Hidden Ground of Love*, p. 45.

p. 14 Ibid., p. 48.

p. 16 *Prayer of the Heart* (The Jesus Prayer) is available on *John Tavener. A Portrait.* NAXOS 8.558152–53, 2004.

p. 16 *The Hidden Ground of Love*, p. 64.

p. 17 Ibid., p. 49.

p. 17 Ibid., p. 57.

p. 18 Ibid., p. 58.

p. 19 *Merton and Sufism. The Untold Story. A Complete Compendium.* Sidney Griffiths, p. 122.

p. 19 Basil Pennington, *Thomas Merton. My Brother.* New City Press, New York, 1996, pp. 114–15.

p. 19 *The Hidden Ground of Love*, p. 63.

p. 20 *The Collected Poems of Thomas Merton. Readings from Ibn Abbad* (1968), New Directions, New York, 1977, p. 745.

p. 20 Surah 50 Qaf v. 16 (Quranic translations listed separately on page 103).

p. 21 See esp. *Mevlana* (trans. 'Our Master) Jalal al-Din Rumi (1207–73) : translated from the Persian by R. A. Nicholson, Unwin, London, 1950. A. J. Arberry *Discourses of Rumi*, S. Weiser, New York, 1972. Anne Marie Schimmel, *Rumi's World*, Shambala, Boston, 2001. Timothy Freke *Rumi Wisdom*, Godsfield Books, Hampshire, 2000. The poem "The Man of God" is a modern adaptation from these sources.

QUTB SOURCES

p. 24 Sayyid Qutb, *In the Shade of the Qur'an. (Fi Zilal al-Qur'an).* Vol. 1, p. 174. Muslim Welfare House, London 1979.

p. 26 Malise Ruthven, *A Fury For God. The Islamist Attack on America.* Granta Books, London 2002, pp. 78–80

p. 26 Ibid., p.81

p. 32 Sayyid Qutb, *In the Shade of the Qur'an*, vol. ii. p. 304.

p. 33 Kenneth Cragg, *The Pen and the Faith.* George Allen & Unwin, London 1985, pp. 53–71.

p. 33 Sayyid Qutb, *Social Justice in Islam,* Cairo, 1954. p. 91.

p. 33 Gilles Kepel, *The Prophet & Pharaoh. Muslim Extremism in Egypt.* Al Saqi Books, London, 1985, p. 41.

p. 33 Sayyid Qutb, *Fiqh al-Din* (Law & Religion). Beirut, 1970. (English Translator and Arabic publisher unidentified).

p. 34 Leonard Binder, *Islamic Liberalism: A Critique of Development Ideologies*. University of Chicago Press, Illinois, 1988, p. 193.

p. 34 Sayyid Qutb, *Fi Zilal al-Qur'an*. In *The Shade of the Qur'an*, Vol. 18. Muslim Welfare House, London 1979. The Islamic Foundation online net, 2004, p. 265.

p. 34 Kenneth Cragg, *The Mind of the Qur'an*. George Allen and Unwin, London 1973, p. 72.

p. 35 Surah 96 Al-'Alaq (Quranic translations listed separately on page 103).

p. 35 *In The Shade of the Qur'an*, Vol. 18, p. 263.

p. 36 *In The Shade of the Qur'an*, Vol. 18, p. 264.

p. 36 *In The Shade of the Qur'an*, Vol. 18, p. 276.

p. 36 *In The Shade of the Qur'an*, Vol. 18, p. 276.

p. 38 *In The Shade of the Qur'an*, Vol. 18, p. 371.

p. 39 <http://www.youngmuslims.ca/online-library/books/milestones>

p. 39 See *Surah Al-Bayyinah* (chapter 98 of the Qur'an, 'The Clear Proof'); *Surah Al-Kafirun* (chapter 109, 'The Unbelievers'); *Surah Al-Ikhlas* (chapter 112 'Purity of Faith'); and *Surah* 9.5. (Quranic translations listed separately on page 103).

p. 39 See. *The Prophet & Pharaoh: Muslim Extremism in Egypt*, p. 42; cf. Zaynab al-Ghazali in *Ayam min Hayati*, Beirut 1979.

p. 40 *A Fury For God. The Islamist Attack on America*, p. 89.

p. 40 Muhammad Asad, *The Message of the Qur'an*. Gibraltar, E.J. Brill, London 1980, p. 256.

p. 40 <http://www.youngmuslims.ca/online-library/books/milestones>; cf. *A Fury For God: The Islamist Attack on America*, pp.90–2.

p. 41 *The Prophet & Pharaoh: Muslim Extremism in Egypt*, p. 38.

p. 41 Gilles Kepel, *The War for Muslim Minds: Islam and the West*. Harvard University Press, Cambridge, Massachusetts, p. 175.

p. 42 Re. Darwin, Freud and Marx, see *In The Shade of the Qur'an*, Vol. 18, p. 320.

p. 42 *In The Shade of the Qur'an*, Vol. 18, p. 345.

p. 42 <http://www.youngmuslims.ca/online-library/books/milestones>

p. 43 <http://www.youngmuslims.ca/online-library/books/milestones>

p. 43 <http://www.youngmuslims.ca/online-library/books/milestones>

p. 43 <http://www.youngmuslims.ca/online-library/books/milestones>

p. 44 <http://www.youngmuslims.ca/online-library/books/milestones>;
cf. *The Prophet & Pharaoh. Muslim Extremism in Egypt*. p.60.

p. 45 Surah 2.256. *Al-Baqarah* (Quranic translations listed separately on page 103).

CRAGG SOURCES

p. 48 Kenneth Cragg, *Sandals at the Mosque: Christian Presence Amid Islam*. SCM Press, London 1959, p. 103.

p. 49 Kenneth Cragg, *Faith and Life Negotiate: A Christian Story-Study*. The Canterbury Press, Norwich, 1994, p. 13

p. 51 Ibid., p.148.

p. 51 Ibid., p. 152.

p. 51 Ibid., p. 278.

p. 52 Ed. A. O'Mahony & M. Kirwan, *World Christianity: Politics, Theology, Dialogues*. Mellisende, London 2004, p. 42.

p. 54 Kenneth Cragg, *The Arab Christian*. John Knox Press, Kentucky 1991, p. 293.

p. 56 Kenneth Cragg, *A Certain Sympathy of Scriptures*. Sussex Academic Press, Brighton & Portland, 2004, pp. xiv & 72.

p. 57 Kenneth Cragg, *Returning to Mount Hira: Islam in Contemporary Terms*. Bellew, London 1994, p.15.

p. 57 Kenneth Cragg, *Readings in the Qur'an*. Collins, London 1988; 2nd edition, Sussex Academic Press, Brighton & Portland 1999, p. 80.

p. 58 Ibid., Preface, p. 10.

p. 58 Kenneth Cragg, *The Christ and the Faiths: Theology in Cross-Reference*. SPCK, London 1986, pp. 344–5.

p. 59 Kenneth Cragg, *The Call of the Minaret*. Oxford University Press, Oxford 1956, Part 2, Chapter 3, p. 63. translates *Fi Manzil al-Wahy* by Muhammad Heikal.

p. 59 Kenneth Cragg, *Muhammad and the Christian*. Darton Longman & Todd (Orbis Books), London and New York, 1984, p. 53.

p. 59 Kenneth Cragg, *Muhammad in the Qur'an: The Task and the Text*. Melisende, London 2001, p. 45.

p. 60 Kenneth Cragg, *Am I Not your Lord? Human Meaning in Divine Question*. Melisende, London 2002. p. 183.

p. 62 *Returning to Mount Hira: Islam in Contemporary Terms*, p. 142.

p. 62 Kenneth Cragg, *Alive to God: Muslim and Christian Prayer*, p. 53.

p. 63 Ibid., p. 55.

p. 63 Ibid., p. 54; cf. Elridge Cleaver, *Soul on Ice*, London 1969, p. 66.

p. 64 *Alive to God: Muslim and Christian Prayer*. p. 55. cf. Colin Turnbull, *The Lonely African*, New York 1962, p. 157.

p. 65 *Alive to God: Muslim and Christian Prayer*. Cf. Introductory Essay, pp. 1–55.

p. 66 Kenneth Cragg, *Semitism: The Whence and Whither*. Sussex Academic Press, Brighton & Portland, 2005, p. 159. Cf. Kenneth Cragg, *This Year in Jerusalem*, 1982 & his *Palestine: The Prize and Price of Zion*, 1997.

p. 66 Ibid., p. 6.

p. 67 Ibid., p.170.

p. 67 Ibid., p.197.

p. 67 Kenneth Cragg, *Poetry of the Word at Christmas*. Churchman Publishing, Worthing, 1987, p. 55.

SARDAR SOURCES

p. 70 Ziauddin Sardar, *British, Muslim, Writer*. Ed. Juliet Steyn, *Other Than Identity: The Subject, Politics and Art*, Manchester University Press, 1996.

p. 73 Ed. S. Inayatullah & G. Boxwell, *Islam, Postmodernism and Other Futures*. Pluto Press, London & Virginia, 2003. Introduction, p. 1.

p. 74 Ziauddin Sardar, *Desperately Seeking Paradise. Journeys of a Sceptical Muslim*. Granta, London 2004, p. 79.

p. 76 Ziauddin Sardar, *Reformist Ideas and Muslim Intellectuals*. From Abdullah Omar Naseef (ed.), *Today's Problems, Tomorrow's Solutions*. Mansell, London 1988, p. 109.

p. 77 Ziauddin Sardar's lecture *Ilm, Islam and the Internet* was unpublished but given at Shakespeare's Globe, London SE1 9DT on Thursday, 25 November 2004.

p. 77 Surah 20.114 *Ta Ha* (O Man). (Quranic translations listed separately on page 103).

p. 78 *Desperately Seeking Paradise*, p. 172.

p. 78 *Islam, Postmodernism and Other Futures*, p. 8.

p. 79 Cf. *Concise Routledge Encyclopaedia of Philosophy*, Routledge, London and New York 2000, pp. 406–10.

p. 80 Seyyed Hossein Nasr, *Man and Nature. The Spiritual Crisis in Modern Man*, Unwin Paperbacks, London 1968, p. 106.

p. 80 *Futures* is published 10 times a year. Ziauddin Sardar is the Editor. *Futures*, 1, Orchard Gate, London NW9 6HU. E-mail: futures@ziasardar.com
A further publication edited by Z. Sardar is Third Text, which is published six times a year: 2G, Crusader House, 249/289, Cricklewood Broadway, London NW2 6NX. E-mail: thirdtext@btopenworld.com

p. 81 Ziauddin Sardar & Zafar Abbas Malik, *Introducing Islam*. Icon Books, Cambridge 1994, p. 43.

p. 81 Surah 1. Al-Fatiha (the Opening). (Quranic translations listed separately on page 103).

p. 82 *Islam, Postmodernism and Other Futures*, p. 178.

p. 83 *Islam, Postmodernism and Other Futures*, pp. 179–80.

p. 83 For *The Rushdie Debate* see: *Desperately Seeking Paradise*, pp. 278–92, 294. *Islam, Postmodernism and Other Futures*, pp. 185, 206, 210, 230–2, 233, 236–7, 240–42. Kenneth Cragg, *Troubled by Truth*, 147–65.

p. 84 For Fay Weldon see *Desperately Seeking Paradise*, pp. 283–6.

p. 85 Ziauddin Sardar and Merryl Wyn Davies, *Why do People Hate America?* Icon Books, Cambridge 2002; <www.iconbooks.co.uk>

p. 86 The popular television series *The West Wing* is examined in *Why do People Hate America?*, pp. 16–22, 24–5, 26–8, 29–33, 36–8.

p. 87 The popular adaptation of the peace prayer of St. Francis appears in *Why do People Hate America*, p. 211.

p. 87 Ziauddin Sardar and Merryl Wyn Davies, *American Dream, Global*

Nightmare. Icon Books, Cambridge 2004. Also available (2005) as CDs by Naxos (5 hours 17 minutes, abridged & read by Merryl Wyn Davies.

p. 87 *The Ten Laws of American Mythology* from *American Dream, Global Nightmare*. pp. 20–7, 239–40.

p. 89 See *Fallujah: Shock & Awe*. Ed. K. Coates. The Spokesman No. 84. Nottingham 2004; <www.russfound.org.uk>

p. 89 Re. Philip Bobbitt, Francis Fukuyama and Samuel Huntington see *American Dream, Global Nightmare*, pp. 214, 215–20, 220–3.

p. 91 Mark Juergensmeyer, *Terror in the Mind of God. The Global Rise of Religious Violence*. University of California Press, Berkeley 2000. See esp. pp. 19–44.

p. 102 Anthony de Mello SJ, *The Prayer of the Frog, Vol. 1*. Anand Press, Gujarat, India 1987, p. 190.

The Qur'an in translation

Orthodox Islam affirms that God's word in the Qur'an is untranslatable. God's choice of the Arabic language for His own *ipsissima verba* is acknowledged. But most people need a translation because only 15 per cent of Muslims know Arabic. The text of the Qur'an available in Arabic, or in any translation today, is that finalised in the caliphate of 'Uthman (644–56). Only a handful of religious texts have exercised a wide and deep influence on the spiritual life of mankind. The Qur'an is such a book.

The first rule of translation is that the translator works in his own first language. This rule rarely applies in English versions of the Qur'an. Three of the translations used in this book were not made by native English speakers. Cragg is translating the Qur'an thematically and not chapter by chapter. English translations of the sacred text of Islam began in the seventeenth century. N. J. Dawood's Penguin Classics version is readily available, alongside the Oxford University Press translation by A. J. Arberry. In order to indicate the nature of variant readings of the original Arabic, the following translations have been used (the last name of the translators is used in parentheses throughout the text):

Abdullah Yusuf Ali, *The Qur'an. Translation and Commentary*, Lahore, Pakistan, 1934, with numerous reprints. Ali was born in 1872. He was educated in India, graduated with a First at Bombay University, read the Law Tripos at Cambridge and was called to the Bar in London, returning home to join the Indian Civil Service. Arabic was one of the passions of his life and his translation of the sacred text, though frequently published without reference to the translator in many Islamic lands, is widely respected. Ali died in London in December 1953. (See M. A. Sherif, *Searching for Solace: A Biography of Abdullah Yusuf Ali. Interpreter of the Qur'an*, Malaysia, 1994).

Muhammad Asad, *The Message of the Qur'an. Translated and explained*. Dar Al-Andalus, Gibraltar 1980. The translator was Leopold Weiss: born in July 1900 in the Austro-Hungarian Empire. He was a Jew from a traditional rabbinical family. In the 1920s he converted to Islam, adopting the name Muhammad in honour of the Prophet and Asad, translated 'lion'. At 80, after seventeen years work, Asad completed his translation and *tafsir* (exegesis, commentary). He died in Spain on 23 February 1992.

Kenneth Cragg, *Readings in the Qur'an*. London 1988; 2nd edition, Brighton & Portland, 1999. Kenneth Cragg has served as an academic and Christian Bishop in the Middle East. He began Arabic studies in the 1930s. This translation is an abridgement but with the intention of conveying the substance of the entire sacred book. The introductory essay is of special value to the reader. The translation is in contemporary English.

M. A. S. Abdel Haleem, *The Qur'an. A new translation*. Oxford University Press, 2004. Professor Haleem heads the department of Islamic Studies at the School of Oriental and African Studies in the University of London. He was born in Egypt and educated at al-Azhar, Cairo and the University of Cambridge. This translation is extraordinarily useful in revealing the serious difficulties involved in translation, especially with regard to the verbal power of Arabic, which is frequently absent from most English versions. The footnotes are of importance in contesting many other translations.

Quranic References

PAGE

Surah 5.82–3	Al-Ma'idah. The Feast (Haleem)	13
Surah 2.152	Al-Baqarah. The Heifer (Ali)	15
Surah 11.114	Hud (named after a prophet)	16-17
Surah 50.16	Qaf (refers to Arabic letter-symbol)	20-1
Surah 96.1–8	Al-'Alaq. The Germ Cell (Asad)	35-6
Surah 109	Al Kafirun. Those who reject faith (Ali)	38
Surah 98	Al-Bayyinah. Clear Evidence (Haleem)	39
Surah 109	Al Kafirun. Those who reject faith (Ali)	39
Surah 112	Al-Ikhlas. Purity of Faith (Haleem)	39
Surah 9	At-Tawbah. Repentance (Asad)	40
Surah 9.5	At-Tawbah. Repentance (Asad)	39
Surah 103	Al-'Asr.The Flight of Time (Asad)	42
Surah 105	Al-Fil. The Elephant (all translations)	42
Surah 2.256	Al-Baqarah. The Heifer (Ali)	45
Surah 17.95	Al-Isra. The Night Journey (Asad)	67
Surah 20.114	Ta Ha. O Man (Asad)	77
Surah 96	Al-'Alaq. The Clinging Form (Haleem)	78
Surah 1	Al-Fatiha. The Opening (Asad)	81

INDEX

Personal Notes

Personal Notes

Personal Notes

Personal Notes

Printed and bound by CPI Group (UK) Ltd, Croydon, CR0 4YY

13/04/2025

14656603-0005